Feisty Aging

Feisty Aging

Hope Wins for Seniors

Cathryn Wellner

Espoir Press
British Columbia
2015

Espoir Press
1002 – 1128 Sunset Drive
Kelowna, British Columbia
Canada V1Y 9W7

Wellner, Cathryn
        Feisty Aging: Hope Wins for Seniors

ISBN 978-0-9939623-3-2

Dedicated to all the wonderful friends who are aging with me. Thanks for taking the fear out of the changes that come with age and for keeping the laughter in my days.

Punctuation and spelling note

I have opted for American spelling since so many of my readers are in the U.S. (The exception is the poem, "The Old Man Hiding in My Mirror", written by a Canadian friend.)

For quotations I have chosen to use what is referred to as "logical placement". If a punctuation mark belongs to the quote, it is placed inside the quotation marks. Otherwise, the punctuation comes afterward. For parenthetical phrases, I use commas only after a longer phrase (5 words or more) or when needed for clarity.

The Old Man Hiding in My Mirror

The glaring light from the string of bulbs above
    the mirror does me no favours.
Apparently, I combed my hair with an egg
    beater this morning.
But, at least I have hair,
My one small victory.
Though who is that stranger in front of me?
My evil twin?
Wrinkles, they must be contagious
I need to stop hanging out with old
    cantankerous curmudgeons
I've caught the virus
Wait! They must be laugh lines
I'm obviously a very funny fellow.

©2013 Rick Hardman

Preface

We know aging is not optional. Still, until we reach milestones that remind us we are closer to death than birth, it is an abstraction.

Then a parent dies. A friend succumbs to cancer. Our travel insurance fees soar because we pass a particular birthday, even though we may be healthier than people much younger. Perfect vision becomes less perfect. Hearing becomes less acute. Mortality whacks us as if we had stepped on a spade and been hit by the handle.

From the moment of conception we begin moving toward the hour of death. But the last chapter can offer incredible riches.

In *Feisty Aging* you will meet inspiring models for finding the treasures in your own aging. You will also find communities, organizations and even countries that value their aging citizens and create programs to enhance life for seniors.

The heroes of these short stories defy the stereotypes that sideline aging citizens in films and on stage. They question the lack of foresight that keeps older people from being considered for jobs or viewed as interesting people with much to contribute.

The seniors you meet here will inspire you to write that book, run that marathon or pursue that dream. You know the one I mean, the one you thought you were too old to contemplate. They will also give you a sense of anticipation, rather than dread, as you consider your own aging.

We age. We die. That much is certain. How we age and how we approach death are up to us, as well as to the societies in which we live.

Sit back. Read. Be inspired. Advocate for change.

While aging is not optional, vibrant aging is. We can age with joy, wisdom and vitality, whatever challenges we may face. We can be role models for those who do not yet understand that feisty aging is possible and a path worth following.

Table of Contents

Part 1 – We Don't Have Time for Bad Days

Life throws us curve balls, but if you count the moments of your life, you will find more to celebrate than to regret.

A Love So True

In 73 years of marriage, Fred and Lorraine Stobaugh never fell out of love. So when the 96-year-old widower heard that Green Shoe Studio in Peoria, Illinois, was holding a singer songwriter contest, he was inspired to pen a song for his beloved, who had died a month before. What Fred lacked in musical talent, he more than made up for in heart-open love.

Officially, Fred's entry did not meet Green Shoe's requirements. Instead of submitting a YouTube video, Fred sent a manila envelope with a letter that said, "I've written a song for my wife." The letter from newly widowed Fred sent an arrow straight into the heart of the Green Shoe team.

They were a new company, hoping to make their mark on the world. The small team had set themselves a big mission, "to change our community one dream at a time." The contest was part of that, an open call to musicians.

Inspired, Fred Stobaugh sat down and wrote a song for the woman who shared his life for more than seven decades. He first saw her at an A&W Root Beer stand, where she was a carhop. That was 1938. Two years later Fred married "the prettiest girl I ever saw."

Lorraine died 75 years later, after a long and loving marriage. Fred missed her. So the 96-year-old man sat down and poured his memories into a love song. The words flowed onto the paper, and he sent them to Green Shoe Studio. Jacob Colgan, Green Shoe's CEO, read them and contacted Fred.

The nonagenarian was hesitant until he understood Green Shoe was offering to produce the song at no cost to him, with a professional singer and backup. The team spent two weeks not only recording the song but also producing a documentary. Fred's story had touched them deeply, and they hoped to fulfill his dream of telling the world about his love.

They posted the video online and were disappointed when it got so little attention. About the time they apologized to Fred for not reaching the world, the video took off. It was watched thousands, then tens of thousands of times a day. Major media got wind of it, and Fred was in demand for interviews. Green Shoe Studio, the fledgling music company, was in the news.

That was 2013. In 2014 Fred Stobaugh came out with a new song, "Took Her Home". The first song, with lines such as "Oh sweet Lorraine, I wish we could do all the good times over again," had brought listeners to tears. The second song, redolent with longing for his wife, dove just as deeply into the warm waters of love with lyrics like these: "I look for the day I can stand by her side."

Fred and Lorraine Stobaugh's love lasted more than seven decades. Thanks to the talented young people at Green Shoe Studio, Fred's tribute to that love will be around for a long time to come.

Read more:

- Green Shoe Studio— http://www.greenshoestudio.com/
- "Sweet Lorraine" video— https://youtu.be/xN8B0gCpi3o
- "Took Her Home" video— https://youtu.be/KEQYMxawO20
- "Fred Stobaugh's 'Oh Sweet Lorraine' Makes iTunes Top 10!"— http://goo.gl/tK6Mek

Decades of Love

During 70 years of marriage, Jack Potter kept a diary. He had always taken notes about his days, but when he met Phyllis Clayson at a wartime dance in 1941, he had even more to write about. That night he fell head over heels in love. She asked him to dance, and they never stopped.

He told the *Daily Mail* he was in the Royal Engineers at the time. When the dance ended, he could not wait to get back home and write, "very nice evening. Danced with very nice girl. Hope to meet her again."

From that day on, he kept brief notes of everyday events in their life as a couple. They married 16 months later. When the war ended, he worked in construction. She worked as a typist.

They had no children, but they had each other, and Jack Potter had his diaries. After 50 years of marriage, Phyllis moved into the Copper Beeches care home in Rochester, Kent, England. Jack visited her every day. When the *Daily Mail* article appeared on March 1, 2013, she was 93, he 91.

Dementia had robbed her of memories. Jack kept them for her in his diaries, adding new bits to share with her. He read them to her and showed her their photographs. He reminisced for her when she could not remember on her own.

They were an unassuming couple, devoted to each other through the decades of their marriage, accepting whatever came their way. At 91, Phyllis Potter was still greeting her husband with open arms when he visited. And Jack still read her the memories her mind could no longer find.

It does not take heroics to change the world, but it does take love. The Potters had plenty of that.

Read more:
- "Devoted Husband Keeps 93-Year-Old Dementia Sufferer Wife's Memories Alive"— http://goo.gl/0TJd23
- "Jack Potter Reads 75 Years of Diaries to Wife With Dementia"— http://goo.gl/7l62sn
- "Diary writer Jack Potter marks meeting the love of his life in diary of 1941"— http://goo.gl/KA4ve3

Becoming Real

There was once a lonely little bear. He arrived along with a beautiful bouquet of flowers on Australian Father's Day 2011. My partner's children grew up in Canada but have made their lives and started their families in Australia. The Aussies honor their dads in early September so the flowers and bear were a double treat, arriving on my birthday.

For a whole year the little bear sat on our bed, waiting for some child to love him. In September 2012 he got his wish. Our youngest grandchild arrived from Melbourne. Within a couple of days she came down with stomach flu. That is when the little bear got a lifetime of snuggles.

When the child felt perky again, the little bear lost out to her favorite stuffed lamb. But that brief time was enough to change the bear, at least for me. He no longer sat alone on the bed. He moved into my office, reminding me of the sweet child who nibbled his ears and cuddled his soft body.

The little bear wasn't hugged long enough to become "Real" in the way *The Velveteen Rabbit* did.

He was hugged long enough to remind me of this passage from Margery Williams's classic.

> "It doesn't happen all at once," said the Skin Horse. "You become. It takes a long time. That's why it doesn't happen often to people who break easily, or have sharp edges, or who have to be carefully kept. Generally, by the time you are Real, most of your hair has been loved off, and your eyes drop out and you get loose in the joints and very shabby. But these things don't matter at all, because once you are Real you can't be ugly, except to people who don't understand."

The words have always moved me, but these days they bring me to tears—not sad tears but tears of gratitude. My grey hair is not as thick as it once was, nor my eyes as sharp. My joints are stiffer than when I was young, and body parts have shifted, sagged and expanded. None of that matters, thanks to people who have loved me through good times and bad. They make me feel Real.

Not everything about aging is easy to embrace. But when we keep our bodies, minds and spirits healthy and remain engaged with life right up to our last breath, we have a good chance of becoming Real. That makes the journey worthwhile.

We Don't Have Time for Bad Days

The time comes when we realize we are past the halfway point in our lives. Bad days are a waste of our remaining hours on this beautiful planet.

David Chase prompted me to think about the implications of those dwindling years. He was leading a service at the Unitarian Fellowship of Kelowna, British Columbia I could not tell you what the rest of the service was about, but I remember clearly his saying, "I'm turning sixty this year. I don't have time for bad days."

A bell rang in my mind. At the time, I was in my late fifties and still in the dumps because of the breakup of my second marriage. I had moved to a town where I knew no one and started a job that had to be created from scratch. I welcomed both the new town and the challenging job, but the settling-in and starting-over phase came with a fair bit of stress. I needed a boost. David's statement was not the only thing that shoved me off the pity path, but it was significant.

It was also prescient. I love that word—from the Latin *prae* (before) and *score* (know)—because his statement was like a verbal crystal ball, offering the vision of good times ahead, but only if I made them good.

Attitude makes a difference. I have done my share of worry and lamentation, but at this stage, looking back is intriguing rather than painful. Instead of regrets I have stories. The experiences made me who I am.

Aging does offer blessings, but the seeds are planted throughout life. So go ahead. However old, or young, you are, plant seeds now that will turn into bright flowers along your path. We have a limited number of years. Some of them will be harder than others. Every one of them will have moments of joy, even the hardest ones.

Life throws us curve balls, but if you count the moments of your life, you will find more to celebrate than to regret.

We don't have time for bad days.

Old People Are Good for the Planet

During our "productive" years in industrial societies, we buy cars and houses and consumer goods. We drive children to ballet lessons and hockey games. Our spending fuels the engines of industry and commerce.

Politicians and economists like that. They tell us we are keeping the economic engine healthy. They count on us to shed cash as quickly as we acquire it, although at the same time they expect us to salt away enough for our retirement.

All that busyness has downsides. Our consumer lifestyles take their toll on the environment. They take their toll on our spirits as well.

So here is the good news. As we age, we live, on average, more lightly on the earth. We commute less, buy fewer new cars, spend less on new clothes, and generally ease up on consumption.

Of course, that is offset by rising health costs...or is it? A lot of pundits claim those of us in the last decades of our lives are an economy-trashing burden. Health care systems are going to crumble under the crush of oldsters competing for nursing care and medical treatments.

The worries are not completely off base. As our bodies edge toward their best-before dates, parts wear out. We are like cars with old engines, brakes, tires and mechanical innards. We start needing more, and more expensive, repairs.

A lot of the expense can be avoided. Housing options that encourage mutual support, such as the Baba Yaga House in France, decrease social isolation, a leading cause of illness and death in older people. So do activity centers where people can drop in, keep fit, and meet new people. Daily exercise and a good diet are also major contributors to healthy aging.

As seniors remain active and involved in their communities, they enjoy more healthy years than earlier generations. The Baby Boom generation may cause some temporary strains because of the population bulge it represents, but in the longer term that will even out. In the interim, aging Boomers offer a wealth of opportunities for intergenerational collaboration and cooperation.

A team of researchers has been examining these issues, using Germany as a case study. The silver lining they discovered in the greying population provides a thoughtful counterpoint to all the fear mongering about aging. Their report, "The Advantages of Demographic Change after the Wave: Fewer and Older, but Healthier, Greener, and More Productive?" appeared in the September 24, 2014 issue of the online journal *PLOS One* and can be read free online.

Aging is not optional. Worrying about it, or fretting over a grey tsunami, is. Read the study (which is in plain language), and relax a little.

Read more:
- "The Advantages of Demographic Change after the Wave"— http://goo.gl/sKOTzI
- "Healthy Naturally Occurring Retirement Communities"— http://goo.gl/k64MwV
- "Healthy Aging Policy Brief"— http://goo.gl/fC5XGL

Living Longer and Better

Dan Buettner came to Kelowna, B.C., to talk about what he called Blue Zones. He was here as part of the University of British Columbia Okanagan's Distinguished Speaker Series. The lecture was in a theater two blocks from our condo.

Buettner's talk made the location seem even better. That same day, we had walked downtown to the Bohemian Cafe to hear Ricardo Scebba talk about his new, story-filled cookbook, *That's Amore.* We had enjoyed a glass of wine and sampled his tasty Pernod prawns while he and his wife, Sue, talked about the restaurant they have operated successfully for the last decade.

That morning we had walked over to the Water Street Senior Centre for the Fitness to Music class. Afterward, a group of us had wandered back to GioBean for coffee and conversation.

A few days earlier we had celebrated Canadian Thanksgiving with a feast that included locally grown vegetables and a free-range turkey. Friends who had gathered around the table were part of our chosen family, people we can count on through the bad times as well as when everything is going fine.

This was all relevant to Dan Buettner's talk. With funding from National Geographic, he spent months researching and writing about the regions with the most centenarians per capita. He found them in five places around the world. After spending time in the communities, doing dozens of interviews, poring over studies, and distilling what he learned, he came up with the Power 9, nine characteristics that seem to be predictors of a long, healthy life. They include such things as living where you can exercise naturally by walking to the store, dropping in on friends or doing your banking. Having a sense of purpose adds up to seven years to our lives. Being part of the "right tribe", people who support healthy behaviors, also adds years.

At the end of the talk, my partner and I agreed we just might live to 100 since we share most of the Power 9 traits. The next morning a friend who had also been at the lecture sent an email that summed up our feeling about it:

> I think we live in one of those 'Blue Zones'. How could it not be so? Length of life aside, it's the quality of life that concerns me. With our adoption of extended family and

supportive friends, we have made our own caring community.

We have found a magical place!

He was right. Like most of our friends, Robin and I definitely exemplify six of the Power 9 and do pretty well on the other three. We just might be around long enough to celebrate a century on the planet.

Check out the Power 9 for yourself. Buettner says if you fit six of the common characteristics of the long-lived people he studied, you just might get twelve more healthy years of life than those without them.

Read more:
- Blue Zones — http://www.bluezones.com/
- Nine predictors of a longer life — http://www.bluezones.com/live-longer/
- "Here Are the Secrets to a Long and Healthy Life"— http://goo.gl/Olw7WN
- "What the 'Blue Zones' Can Teach Us about Living Longer"— http://goo.gl/5K7eNL

Part 2 - Creative to the End

"Boats" by acclaimed artist Hilda Gorenstein is evidence that the spark of creativity lights our lives at every stage. When progressive memory loss threw challenges in her way, her daughter asked if she would like to paint again. She replied, "Yes, I remember better when I paint."

The Joy Lives On

Hilda Gorenstein was a gifted artist. Born in Montreal in 1905, she grew up in Portland, Oregon and graduated from Chicago's School of the Art Institute. To avoid the prejudice against women artists, she signed her works, "Hilgos". Her watercolors, oils, acrylics, sculptures and drawings were exhibited across the United States. Buyers added them to collections around the world.

But success can never insure us against the vicissitudes of aging. For Gorenstein, life's little erosions turned major when she was diagnosed with progressive memory loss. As her symptoms worsened, her daughter, Berna Huebner, asked if she would like to paint again. She responded, "Yes, I remember better when I paint."

On the advice of Dr. Lawrence Lazarus, a geriatric psychiatrist at Rush-Presbyterian-St. Luke's Medical Center, Huebner contacted the School of the Art Institute. They agreed to connect Gorenstein with students. The result was extraordinary.

Although she had retreated ever further into a world no one else could enter, she was still an artist. When students handed her brushes dipped in paint, she would lean into the work, creating works so colorful and alive no one could doubt she still lived and breathed art. Other times she needed no prompting to begin painting.

With paint brush in hand, Gorenstein's dark cloud of severe memory loss lifted. Her spirits brightened as she added stroke after stroke to nautical scenes and abstract art.

After Gorenstein's death, family and friends started the Hilgos Foundation to provide scholarships for students at the School of the Art Institute of Chicago. Inspired by the impact of art on her mother, Berna Huebner created *I Remember Better When I Paint,* a documentary narrated by Olivia de Havilland and co-produced by French Connection Films and the Hilgos Foundation. She also published a book with the same title. Both are "about the positive impact of art and other creative therapies on people with Alzheimer's and how these approaches can change the way we look at the disease."

We can feel helpless watching friends or family members disappear into the swirling fog of Alzheimer's. What Hilda Gorenstein taught us was that the human spirit is still reachable if we can find the keys. For some that is painting. For others it might be music or dance.

Huebner's documentary and book are inspiring reminders that people with Alzheimer's can still sparkle when the parts of the brain still functioning well are engaged in creative activities. The stigma of dementia will ease when we learn to focus on gifts instead of deficits.

Read more:

- Hilgos Foundation—
  http://www.hilgos.org/main.html
- "Owning our Health: I Remember Better When I Paint"— http://goo.gl/DGAncx
- "'I Remember Better When I Paint': Treating Alzheimer's Through the Creative Arts" documentary website—https://goo.gl/qQvxVH

Creative at Any Age

First it was the germ of an idea. Then it was a collaborative effort. Now *Sage-ing with Creative Spirit, Grace and Gratitude* is a full-blown, online, quarterly magazine, a feast for eye and spirit and a boost to healthy aging.

Karen Close dreamed it into being. Robert MacDonald, the visionary behind Okanagan Institute, brought all the strands together into its online form.

The first edition launched September 22, 2011, at the Okanagan Institute's Express series in Kelowna, B.C. Five of the contributors, including Karen, shared a piece of what it is that so tickles their spirit they have to scratch it by painting, writing, drawing, or making music. Though Karen, Ruth Bieber, Carolyn Cowan, Sandy McNolty, and Brenda Valnicek each followed a different Muse, they all had at least three things in common. First, they shared the passion and courage to create. Second, they were Boomers, at varying points of that population bulge. Third, they were proud to have their work featured in such a high-quality publication.

Sage-ing with Creative Spirit, Grace and Gratitude is "for all those serious in exploring their creativity, in a chosen expression. It is a forum for publication and exposure to other artists, both novice and established. The journal is an easel for any form of artistry undertaken out of personal intuition and imagination."

Being part of the journal has encouraged contributors to explore, and believe in, their own creative passions. *Sage-ing* is an invitation to engage in the dance of creativity.

Full disclosure: I am proud to have articles in Issue 7 and Issue 12 and to have one of my pieces included in *Creative Aging*, the beautiful book that grew out of the journal.

Read more:
- *Sage-ing with Creative Spirit, Grace and Gratitude*— http://sage-ing.com/
- Okanagan Institute— http://okanaganinstitute.com/
- Creative Aging— http://goo.gl/Mh5yXw

Poetry Bestseller at 99

Toyo Shibata was 92 when she reluctantly gave up classical dancing. She was not ready to be idle. She needed an outlet for her creative energy. Her son suggested poetry.

She began writing poems. When a newspaper published one, she knew she had found her niche.

By the time her story hit the international media, her first anthology, *Kujikenaide (Don't Lose Heart)* had become a stunning success story. The book started out as a self-published title. She already had a large audience when the publisher Asuka Shinsha approached her. They produced an illustrated version and sold over 1.5 million copies.

In his article for *Huffington Post*, John Lundberg wrote the book had reached a Japanese audience "tired of two decades of recession and thirsting for the wisdom of experience."

Experience is what Shibata gave them. Her poems were full of her joy in daily life and her keen observations on growing old.

As she neared her 100th birthday, Toyo Shibata was still writing poetry. She died in a Tokyo nursing home in 2013, at the age of 101. By then her book had been translated into numerous languages and had been followed by a second anthology, *Hyakusai (100 Years Old)*.

We are all thirsting for wisdom, along with meaning and hope. If you dream of writing a work that touches hearts, taking a photograph that makes viewers gasp or painting a picture that enlarges spirits, keep creating. Your work may be exactly what someone needs.

Read more:
- "Toya Shibata, Japanese Grandma, Is Bestselling Author At 99"— http://goo.gl/TAKhnu
- "Grandma poet is dead at 101"— http://goo.gl/Kn8Ih4
- "'Grandma next door' poet a Japan bestseller at 99"— http://goo.gl/UNVA2a

First-time, Prize-winning Novelist at 78

Jamil Ahmad, a first-time novelist from Pakistan, made the 2011 shortlist for the Man Asian Literary Prize with *The Wandering Falcon*. The book was a collection of linked short stories he finished, then tucked in a drawer, in 1974.

In 2008 his younger brother urged him to submit the manuscript to a competition for Pakistani authors. Ahmad edited the stories and sent the manuscript to Faiza Sultan Khan, a Karachi columnist and editor. Khan showed it to an editor at Penguin. Two years later the work was published. Nearly four decades after he drafted the book, the 78-year-old, retired civil servant received the prestigious Shakti Bhatt First Book Prize.

And what a book it is. *The Wandering Falcon* takes readers into the wildly beautiful tribal borderlands of Afghanistan and Pakistan. The story begins with a young couple forced to flee when they defy tradition and their families' wishes by falling in love. Our guide is Tor Baz, son of the ill-fated couple, a mysterious wanderer whose interactions draw readers into the lives of those he meets.

In 2014, only a few years after his publishing success, the 83-year-old author died. His account of experiences as a Pakistani civil servant in tribal lands had become a bestseller.

The book you wrote but have not yet published, the dance you choreographed but have not performed, the lyrics you polished but have not yet been sung may harbor the seeds of greatness. Is it languishing in a drawer, a reminder of youthful dreams you only re-visit when you are moving from one house to another?

Take it out, polish it, and let it see the light of day. You may be the next Jamil Ahmad.

Read more:
- "Jamil Ahmad, Who Published Debut Novel at 79, Dies at 83" — http://goo.gl/cciyCQ
- "Pakistan's Unlikely Storyteller of the Swat Valley" — http://goo.gl/hsnDXK
- "Five Questions for: Author Jamil Ahmad" — http://goo.gl/RK9Epz

Little House Books Author Got Late Start

When she began writing the books that would become one of the most successful children's series of all time, Laura Ingalls Wilder was 65. Her homesteading family had not been out of the ordinary in the heartland of late-1800s America. What made her fictional accounts of their lives into best-selling books was Wilder's ability to turn ordinary family life into compelling stories.

Other women lived through blizzards, survived hunger times, became teachers when they were barely older than their students, and lost siblings and parents to accidents and illnesses. But few who put pen to paper to record their lives had Wilder's gift for turning everyday troubles and joys into something both exceptional and universal.

In the mid-1920s, when Wilder was nearing her 60th birthday, her daughter Rose began nudging her to write down her childhood stories. The result was *Pioneer Girl*, which Rose edited.

Publishers yawned and turned it down. Undaunted, Wilder changed the voice from first to third person, added more happy-family stories, and re-wrote it for children. In 1932 it was published as *Little House in the Big Woods.*

The book touched the hearts of young readers and their parents. It was 1932, and Wilder was suddenly a 65-year-old, successful author. She kept writing and did not stop until she completed her eighth Little House book.

Despite Wilder's keen eye for a good story, she might never have published her enduring series without her daughter's encouragement, editing, and publishing contacts. Her success was both a personal triumph and a satisfying family story. Generations of children are happier for it.

Read more:
- "Wilder Women: The Mother and Daughter behind the Little House Stories" — http://goo.gl/pckVDJ
- "Little Libertarians on the Prairie" — http://goo.gl/edyzY3
- "*Pioneer Girl* by Laura Ingalls Wilder Review – Gritty Memoir Dispells Little House Myths" — http://goo.gl/kMiWFu

Boyd Lee Dunlop's Buffalo Blues

If photojournalist Brendan Bannon had not stopped by a nursing home to talk with a doctor about a project, Boyd Lee Dunlop might have died without recording his music.

Dunlop had been a musician from the time he acquired his first piano, a broken-down instrument found outside his house. His aunt was a violinist with the Buffalo Philharmonic Orchestra. His brother Frankie became a well-known drummer. Dunlop found work in the steel mills and rail yards of Buffalo.

He kept playing piano and became a regular in clubs around his city. Music was his soul's work, but he never became known outside the club circuit.

Eventually he went into a Buffalo, New York, nursing home. One day Brendan Bannon showed up and talked with him. The aging pianist offered to play for him. The sounds the old man brought out of the dilapidated instrument in the cafeteria set in motion the chain of events that led to the 85-year-old musician's recording his first album, *Boyd's Blues*, with the help of producer Allen Farmelo. Soon after, he recorded a second album, *The Lake Reflections*.

When Dunlop died in 2013, fellow musicians honored him with a jazz jam at Buffalo's Colored Musicians Club. His passing was mourned by many, who recognized him for the jazz master he was.

The music had always been there, in Dunlop's bones and soul, but it would not be here now without an accidental meeting in the Delaware, a nursing home in Buffalo, New York.

Read more:
- "A Jazz Pianist Gets His Big Break - at Age 85"— http://goo.gl/q6kuQK
- "Rhythms Flow as Aging Pianist Finds New Audience" — http://goo.gl/7WPN7B
- "Boyd Lee Dunlop: Solo Piano" — http://goo.gl/7YyfF1

Her First CD at 78

No, that is not 78 rpm (revolutions per minute), which people of a certain age will recognize as industry standard for early disc recordings. This 78 refers to the age of Langley, B.C. singer, Shirley Buchan. At 78 she released her first recording, a collection of jazz and torch songs she called, *Standing in the Centre of My Dreams.*

I learned about Buchan when I watched an Express episode shot by Shaw (a cable company). The second story was about a woman who, at the age of seven, knew singing was her destiny.

Life got in the way. She was 71 when she decided it was not too late. She formed a group called "Part & Parcel Singers", whose beautiful harmonies you can hear on the video and the CD. (The links are at the end of this post.)

Becoming a recording artist was not Buchan's first re-invention. At 50 she took up fitness and enjoyed it so much she was still teaching classes when she recorded her album. When she was in her mid-70s, she visited Africa for the first time. In

Kenya she dived into a project to assist women and children. She will very likely still be trying new things every year of the rest of her life.

If you hear yourself thinking, "I'm too old to...," watch Shirley Buchan, and go do whatever it is you think you can't. If you need more of a kick in the pants, keep reading. Let the stories in this book change those limiting beliefs that keep you from forging ahead with your dreams.

Read more:

- The Express on location in Langley, May 11, 2011 —https://youtu.be/e6A_34Pjk7Y
- Shirley Buchan on CDBaby — http://www.cdbaby.com/Artist/ShirleyBuchan

The Old Violinist

The old man was one seat away from me in the Williams Lake, B.C., airport. At his side was a battered violin case.

"Do you play violin or fiddle?" I asked.

"Both," he said. "I entertained the troops with it back in World War II."

We had time, and he had a story. He was a young Canadian soldier, stationed in Brighton. He walked into the pawnshop on a lark. "How much for the violin?" he asked.

The shop owner wanted 25 pounds. The soldier did not have that much money.

A soldier's pay was $1.25 a day. In those days the pound was worth five Canadian dollars. He could never save enough to buy the violin, not in the time he would be in Brighton.

"It took me three weeks to talk her down," he said. He had finally found the magic words: "I want the violin to entertain the troops."

The shopkeeper's husband was a soldier. Maybe the young Canadian would lift his spirits one day.

"Fifteen pounds," she said, and the soldier walked out with the violin.

He was shipped off to battle. He would tuck the violin in the storage compartment at the bottom of the tank, where it stayed safe through battles. Unless they were under fire, he would pull it out at every stop. He played for the troops. He played for civilians. He played for the life back home and for the peace he wished for the war-torn lands.

Fifty years later the memories were still fresh. "Do you want to hear a tune?" he asked.

I nodded, and he took out his violin. It still bore the tassel from which it had hung on the pawnshop wall.

There in the crowded, airport waiting room he played "Lily Marlene" and "White Cliffs of Dover", "It's a Long Way to Tipperary" and "The Boogie Woogie Bugle Boy". He played his memories of blood and horror, of ragged dreams and eventual homecoming.

After half a dozen songs, he lowered the violin. There was a smattering of polite applause. The man was no great talent, but his music was true and clear. It took him back to battlefields, frightened civilians, and fallen comrades.

As he returned the scratched violin to its battered case, I asked if he felt the violin had brought him luck.

"Yes," he said softly, as he gently placed the instrument back in its case. "It brought me through."

In war-torn Europe he played music for the ear and for the soul. It was a small gesture of normalcy, of pleasure in a time of war.

The violinist was a small man, perhaps five feet tall, thin, grey-haired, dressed in black. But his heart was large, and he shared a piece of it as we all waited for our flights to be called.

It's Not Over Till the Old Lady Dances

Sarah Patricia "Paddy" Jones began dancing when she was two and a half years old. In spite of the joy it gave her, she stopped dancing when she married at the age of 22. She and her husband reared four children in England, then moved to Spain in 2001, when her husband David retired. After less than two years in their new home, David died of leukemia.

The best way to deal with loss can be to try something new and exciting. For Jones the adventure was flamenco dancing. She enrolled in Nico Espinosa's dance school. When she mastered salsa, she and her teacher decided to become a dance duo.

This was not just a whim. It was a passion. Nico's lessons took her farther than most 80-year-olds would dare go. She and Nico became a dancing duo. In 2009 they entered Tú sí que vales, a Spanish talent show. Spurred by their win of a significant sum of money, they tried their dance moves in Argentina.

The two were voted off the show in the eleventh round. Tension between the pair led to an end of their duo.

Somehow they patched it up. In 2014 they won the hearts of audience and judges in Britain's Got Talent. The pair went straight from first appearance to the semi-finals, where they came in ninth.

Their official Facebook page shows no activity since the British talent show, but it hardly matters. Paddy Jones's stardom was a dream deferred, but it was a dream attained.

Read more:
- "Paddy Jones, Salsa-Dancing 75-Year-Old British Granny, Wins Spanish Talent Show"— http://goo.gl/OtTSUI
- "Britain's Got Talent's 79-Year-Old Dancing Star Is a Lesson to Us All"— http://goo.gl/QhekFz
- "Interview: Paddy Jones, Britains [sic] Got Talent"— http://goo.gl/TFgSqI

Janey Cutler Had No Regrets

Janey Cutler was 80 years old when she stepped onto the stage of Britain's Got Talent (BGT) and knocked the socks off the judges. The Glaswegian great-grandmother had been entertaining in local pubs and clubs since rearing her seven children. When friends talked her into auditioning for the popular show, she chose the perfect song, the English version of Charles Dumont's and Michel Vaucaire's famous "Non, je ne regrette rien".

As always happens in the particularly heartwarming episodes of these talent shows, judges' faces lit up and the audience went wild when the elderly woman began to sing. Cutler's powerhouse, lived-in voice rocked the hall. When Simon Cowell asked her how many years she had waited to do that, she replied, "I'm just thankful I am here tonight."

Chosen as one of the finalists, Cutler was compared to Susan Boyle, who had shot to stardom on the show. Cutler went on to the BGT finals, toured Britain with the top talent and even recorded an album with the Chelsea Pensioners.

She became a media darling, interviewed by newspapers, appearing on television and meeting some of her entertainment idols. She finished ninth in the finals and then happily retired to her cozy home, basking in the memories. At 82 she died in her sleep.

Cutler's time in the spotlight was a short but blazing finale to her life. She died a happy woman, with the courage to pursue a dream at an age when most would say, "I'm too old."

She could say with conviction, "I have no regrets."

Read more:
- "Britain's Got Talent Singer Janey Cutler Dies at 82"— http://goo.gl/pmQJyA
- "'New Susan Boyle' Janey Cutler Set for Global Fame after Wowing Britain's Got Talent Judges" — http://goo.gl/GzLYzd
- "Singing Scots Grandmother Janey Cutler in Talent Final"— http://goo.gl/U5sZpO

Six Fabulous Fashionistas

The six models in Sue Bourne's *Fabulous Fashionistas* documentary have a strong sense of personal style. Ranging in age from 73 to 91 at the time of the filming, they were determined not to go blandly into that good night.

Bourne, an award-winning producer/director, explored aging with style through the stories of Bridget, Sue, Daphne, Jean, Gillian and Lady Trumpington. This was not her first foray into the land of the aging. In her 2001 documentary, *Bus Pass Bandits*, she explored the shady world of criminal pensioners. Both films show Bourne's fascination with the nose-thumbing world of senior citizens who don't give two cents for ordinary conventions.

Finding the six fashionistas was not easy. There was no directory of fabulously stylish older women. Hoping to find inspiration for her own aging, Bourne went in search of them. She preferred women whose years showed, without Botox or plastic surgery, but who were models for aging with style. The six she found fit that bill.

The six Fabulous Fashionistas were stylish to the core, but there was nothing conventional about them. Each was fiercely individual. Daphne Selfe was the oldest model in Britain and was re-discovered at 70, after her husband's death. Gillian Lynne, born in 1926, was still choreographing major productions. Lady Trumpington was a Conservative member of the House of Lords. Sue Kreitzman enjoyed a successful career as a food writer until, in 1998, she began focusing on drawing, painting and building assemblages. Jean Woods worked in a trendy boutique in Bath and ran three times a week. Bridget Sojourner was a life-long activist and charity-shop sleuth, adept at finding stylish treasures at bargain prices.

Bourne treated them with respect in her film, portraying them as women with spark and originality rather than as eccentric old ladies. That was the real strength of the documentary, more than the age of the models. These women did not begin to be vibrant when they hit some magic age society defines as old. They were already Fabulous Fashionistas. Now they were also old.

Western cultures shelve older women, painting them invisible from menopause, or even before, onward. The six women in Bourne's documentary refused to quietly fade away or to let anyone else define them. They were aging with zest and spirit, giving the world their own definitions of what it means to grow old.

Read more:

- "Don't Dress Your Age: Six Women Say No to Drab"— http://goo.gl/L0Ucfj
- "Why I Created Fabulous Fashionistas – an Interview with Film Maker Sue Bourne"— http://goo.gl/XwQjnc
- "'Fabulous Fashionistas' Review – Six Ladies' Love of Life Provides Inspiration for Viewers of All Ages"— http://goo.gl/eSd4x9

Dream Job at 91

If a company wanted to design high-tech gadgets for the elderly, they would be smart to get advice from someone old enough to understand the landscape of aging. That is what IDEO did when the company connected with 90-year-old Barbara Beskind.

IDEO is well known for innovative design. When they turned their attention to an aging population, they sought firsthand knowledge of challenges and needs faced by the elderly. The 90-year-old Beskind applied and was hired.

Her design career began when she was only eight. It was the Depression. Toys were in short supply. Only by creative use of found materials could she and her mates have the playthings they wanted. Beskind turned to a supply that was freely available, old tires. She turned them into hobby horses for herself and her playmates.

Her interest in design never flagged, though she ran into barriers. When she graduated from high school, she was told girls could not enroll in engineering courses. So she turned a home economics degree into a career as an occupational therapist. That career handed her design opportunities. Developing therapeutic technology for people with balance problems (and receiving six patents) gave her the right set of skills when IDEO began searching for someone to assist them with designing for seniors. The advice turned into a one day a week job.

Beskind not only had personal experience with aging. She was a keen observer. She had moved into a retirement community and seen the challenges faced by her contemporaries. That gave her ideas very useful to IDEO.

For instance, she witnessed a lot of falls and their aftermaths. That prompted her to design a sort of airbag for walkers, one that would deploy with a 15-degree lurch. For people having trouble remembering names, she designed eyeglasses with cameras and speakers. They recorded photos and names as people introduced themselves to the eyeglass wearer and then discretely identified that person the next time he met them.

Age is not the defining factor for intelligence and creativity. IDEO recognized the gifts Beskind brought to design and gave her the opportunity to contribute her creative intelligence. As for Barbara

Beskind, she is a beacon for healthy aging and has said she is living one of the best chapters of her life.

Read more:
- "At 90, She's Designing Tech for Aging Boomers"— http://goo.gl/UT86sA
- "In 'Ageist' Silicon Valley, 90-Year-Old Designer Happy at IDEO"— http://goo.gl/80uYat
- "91-Year-Old Is Living Her Dream as a Tech Designer at Silicon Valley Firm"— http://goo.gl/Zr9ASy

Part 3 - A Bridge between Old and Young

Building bridges between young and old shatters stereotypes, dispels fears, increases understanding, and spreads a whole lot of joy.

Teenagers Return an Old Woman's Love

A wave and a smile seemed such a small thing to offer high school students, but they noticed, and they figured out a way to thank Tinney Davidson. She and her husband Ken moved to Comox, B.C., in 2007. Sitting in the window of their living room, they began to wave at students walking to and from Highland Secondary School.

Young people found themselves looking forward to the friendly smiles and waves. They began watching for the Davidsons each day.

Most were content with waving. A few stopped to introduce themselves. One of them, Ginger Long, brought Tinney a cupcake. Some of the students began visiting.

When Ken died, Tinney continued her daily smile vigil. She also knitted hats. She had been knitting the colorful hats since her granddaughter's bout of cancer treatments, hoping they would cheer the girl if she lost her hair. Her granddaughter knitting the colorful hats since her granddaughter's bout of cancer treatments, hoping they would cheer the girl if she lost her hair. Her granddaughter survived. Tinney kept knitting. She sold the hats to passersby and donated the money to the hospital.

Students were touched by her warmth and generosity. As Valentine's Day 2014 neared, one of them said to math teacher Charlotte Hood-Tanner, "Ms. Tanner, there is a really cool lady who lives down the street who sells hats for cancer. What should we do?"

They decided to honor the 84-year-old at a school assembly. They made a video for her, painted a banner and made cards. They even brought in the chair she always sits in. Davidson was overwhelmed, seeing how much her smiles had brightened the lives of students passing by her house.

To her it was a daily pleasure, smiling and waving at passing students. To the students it was an unexpected kindness. They will remember her. One day they will pass the story on to their children. Some will be inspired to do their own good deeds for others because of Tinney Davidson.

Read more:
- "84-Year-Old Woman Who Waves to Students Each Day Gets a Valentine's Day Surprise"— http://goo.gl/5178mM

- "Small Gestures Go a Long Way"—
  http://goo.gl/IZFFv8
- "Comox School Honours 'Really Cool Lady'"—
  http://goo.gl/VwSXg3

Facebook and an Aging Street Poet

Hope is the heaviest weight
A man can carry
It is the bane of the idealist
~ The Conditioned

He was just another homeless old man on the streets of São Paolo, surrounded by the detritus of his humble existence. He might have ended his life that way. Then something changed. Thanks to a kind-hearted young woman and the power of a good story, Raimundo Arruda Sobrinho achieved his dream of becoming a published poet.

Born in 1938, Raimundo had been a gardener and bookseller. He was educated and well spoken. Even when he ended up homeless on the streets of São Paolo, he wrote every day. For more than three decades, he survived with no home and no security. Wrapped in plastic bags, he penned his poems, signing each, "The Conditioned". He gave them freely to any passerby who showed interest.

One day a young woman, Shalla Monteiro, stopped to talk with him. He gave her a poem. She came back again and again. He shared his dream of publishing his poems. She started a Facebook page to bring his work to a larger audience.

Many visited the page and were inspired. Then something even better happened. Thanks to Monteiro and Facebook, Raimundo's family learned of his whereabouts and reconnected with him. His younger brother, sister and nephews gave him a home and a place to belong. The old poet continued his daily writing, but now his work was regularly available to an expanding audience.

His online trail seems to end after April 2014. Perhaps he is still writing, perhaps not. That he survived nearly 35 years on the streets of São Paolo, writing constantly, is a testament to the human spirit. The grizzled, homeless man was a talented poet. Nothing stopped him from writing, but it took a compassionate and determined young woman to fulfill his dream of publishing his poems. And it took Facebook to return him to his family.

Read more:
- "How a Woman's Kindness and Facebook Helped a Homeless Poet Find His Family and a New Start"— http://goo.gl/SenjPS
- Official blog for Raimundo Arruda Sobrinho — http://ocondicionado.blogspot.it/

Kids Make the Age Pie Bigger

When Revera (now Comfort Life) partnered with Reel Youth on an intergenerational project, *Age Is More*, they were determined to combat a form of social prejudice that is cruelly prevalent and widely tolerated: ageism. Just how much this is needed was made clear in the 2012 Revera Report on Ageism. It revealed some disturbing attitudes among Canadians, such as these:

- 63% of seniors 66 years of age and older say they have been treated unfairly or differently because of their age
- 35% of Canadians admit they have treated someone differently because of their age
- 51% of Canadians agree ageism is the most tolerated social prejudice when compared to gender- or race-based discrimination
- 79% of Canadians agree that seniors 75 and older are seen as less important and are more often ignored than younger generations

- 71% agree that Canadian society values younger generations more than older generations
- 21% of Canadians say older Canadians are a burden on society.

That kind of prejudice leads to some nasty social consequences, including a sense of isolation and irrelevance for people with years of accumulated expertise and accomplishments to share.

The project was an eye opener for the young filmmakers, as you can see in the *Age Is More* films from Burlington, Ontario, and White Rock, British Columbia. They met people who challenged their stereotypes, such as Bernie Custis (retired school principal and first black quarterback in North American professional football), Dilys Mary Shotton (who at 91 still had "riding an elephant" on her bucket list) and Lisa McCue (an artist who set out on a freighter at a time when young girls generally did not do things like that).

The findings of the Revera survey and all the hand wringing about the "grey tsunami" are cause for dismay. Pitting people against each other by age groupings is small-pie thinking, the kind that decides life is one small pie. If you get a piece, I don't.

Life does not work that way. The pie gets larger when we are open to the contributions of people of any age, gender, culture, differing abilities, and whatever other designations we use to categorize people. *Age Is More* was designed to enlarge the pie for the young and old who participated and for anyone else open to a bit of mind changing.

Read more:
- Revera Report on Ageism — http://goo.gl/aWbGul
- Age Is More videos — http://reelyouth.ca/ageismore_appleby.html
- Revera's *Age Is More* website http://goo.gl/rROFbq

Canadian Soccer Stars in a Maryland Retirement Home

When two Canadian soccer stars moved into the Ingleside at King Farm retirement community in Rockville, Maryland, they were greeted like the stars they were on the field. David Gutnick recorded an audio documentary about them for CBC. In it he pointed out the symmetry in average ages at Ingleside: 28 for the young women, 82 for the elderly residents.

Robyn Gayle and Diana Matheson were at the top of their sport. They had their moment in the sun at the 2012 Olympics, when the Canadian women's soccer team took home bronze. Then they played with Washington Spirit, as part of the National Women's Soccer League.

There are, however, no 7-figure contracts in this league so an offer of a condo in a retirement community felt like a gift from heaven to the young women. It was also a gift for their retired neighbors, who went out of their way to embrace the athletes. The residence even scheduled a shuttle bus so seniors could support the women's home games.

The arrangement came out of a conversation Ingleside's vice-president of marketing had with the executive director, Marilyn Leist. At first, Leist said, "I looked at her like she had three heads because I thought she was nuts." Once she gave the idea some thought, Leist saw it as a model for other intergenerational housing schemes.

Ingleside recognized that integrating generations had benefits for young and old. The soccer players discovered that old people were richly diverse and interesting. The elderly residents learned a lot about soccer. Having the young women around boosted their spirits.

Isolating people by age groupings is unnatural and unhealthy. One day we may look back on retirement communities and nursing homes as relics of an unenlightened past.

Read more:
- "Canadian Women's Soccer Stars Shake Up U.S. Retirement Home"— http://goo.gl/upUqKy
- "Washington Spirit Players Living at Rockville Retirement Community"— http://goo.gl/0XQA27

Seniors Connect Via Social Media

Some of the most vibrant people around have been on the planet so many decades they are like walking history lessons. They have lived through a speeded-up period of change. Had they fallen asleep in their twenties and awakened in the 21st century, they would probably have figured they had been through a time warp.

They may not be digital natives, but they have passports to techno-land and are embracing the new land of social media. Brett Blair and Hope Hickli recorded the phenomenon in a research/outreach project called "Seniors Connected." In partnership with the Alexander Mackie Assisted Living Residence in Langford, B.C., they tested the impact of social media on high-functioning seniors' cognitive function and social connections.

Not surprisingly, the effect was positive. The grey-hair and wrinkles brigade is becoming far more digitally competent than a lot of younger people realize. A 2013 study by Pew Research Center showed that only one percent of seniors 65 and older used social networking sites in May 2008. By May 2013 that number had increased to 43 percent.

While that is still less than half, it represents huge growth in five years. In the past, seniors who had to pare their belongings and shoehorn themselves into assisted-living homes found themselves cut off from the outside world. Computers and social media have changed that dreary picture.

A project like this one is the tip of the intergenerational iceberg. It can take the fear out of aging, for both old and young. Kudos to Blair and Hickli for calling on more seniors' residences to enter the digital age.

Read more:
- "Seniors Connected" video — https://youtu.be/R4F6CX73RS8
- "A Film & Study on the Impact of Social Media on Seniors"— http://goo.gl/1bRUk4

Youth Teach the Old in Mentor Up

The premise behind Mentor Up is simple: You know it. They need it.

AARP, the American Association of Retired People, knows a lot of older people are stumped by the dizzying advances in technology. At the same time, younger people are born into the technology maelstrom and adapt easily to constant change. So AARP started Mentor Up to link digital immigrants with digital natives.

The intergenerational program gives young people a chance to mentor older people. By sharing their technology expertise, youth teach older people how to use social media, connect with far-off friends and relatives, find or create jobs, and become comfortable in the digital world.

The reverse mentoring program works through existing organizations and institutions. For example, Carmel High School in California has a "Wired for Connections/Mentor Up" club. It was launched by

16-year-old Sean Butler, who offered 45-minute mentoring sessions for members of the Carmel Foundation. When classmate Carly Rudiger joined him, she expanded his idea into a club whose members earn community-service credits by mentoring.

Mentor Up is a natural way of connecting generations. Children growing up today have never known a world in which tablets, smart phones and computers were something new or unfamiliar. The young tutors in Mentor Up have no fear of totally messing things up. They make the perfect teachers for wary seniors.

Before they start mentoring, volunteers go through sensitivity training so they can understand some of the frustrations older people face, such as failing eyesight, loss of dexterity, or lack of basic familiarity with digital devices. The results are a boost for both sides of the learning equation.

Not every Mentor Up program is technology focused. Some connect the generations around meals. Others provide companions to elders or train youth to encourage basic fitness among seniors. The Mentor Up site offers lots of downloadable resources that can help groups get started.

The value of Mentor Up goes well beyond the digital divide. It allows generations divided by decades to discover their commonalities.

Read more:
- Mentor Up website — https://www.mentorup.org/
- "Confused by Tech? Kids to the Rescue"— http://states.aarp.org/co-mentor/
- "Bridging the Digital Divide: MSU Denver Students Mentor AARP Members with Technology Lessons"— http://goo.gl/NcipTB

The 90-year-old Primary Student

Priscilla Sitienei has brought babies into the world for 65 years. Now she wants to do something more for children. The Kenyan woman, who is in her 90s, wants to inspire them.

To do so she has become the oldest primary school student in the world. Six of her own great-great-grandchildren are in class with her.

By modeling how important education is to her, the great-great-grandmother believes she can encourage children to go to school. When the woman her classmates call "Gogo" (grandmother) sees children who are not in school, she asks them why. If they tell her they are too old, she points to her own example.

Priscilla Sitienei joins in the children's activities. She helps them with their school work. She passes on the stories and traditions of her people.

When she first approached the school and asked to enroll, Sitienei was met with skepticism. She would not give up on the idea. She was determined to be able to read the Bible on her own. She also wanted to learn to write so she could pass on her mastery of midwifery and traditional medicines. She insisted she belonged in school. Her persistence wore down the skeptics, and she enrolled.

While she learns, the elderly scholar inspires her young classmates, school staff, and anyone else who hears her story. School is a better place for everyone, with Priscilla Sitienei's wise influence.

Read more:

- "Kenyan Grandmother at School with Her Great-Great-Grandchildren"—http://goo.gl/Ns8X1z
- "90 Year Old Granny in School" video — https://youtu.be/FVkys_RTpxk
- "This 90-Year-Old Kenyan Goes to Primary School with Her Great-Great-Grandchildren"—http://goo.gl/2ihCQA

Soup's on at NANA

Warmth and welcome were on offer at NANA, "a comfort food and craft cafe run by older ladies" from the area around Clapton in the UK. It started as a pop-up café in a pub they rented for five hours a day. Then they leased an old public toilet, renovated it, and set up shop.

A Kickstarter campaign got them enough funds to install a commercial kitchen and the other amenities required by a restaurant. As part of offering comfort to the community, they also re-opened the public toilets.

The idea came from Katie Harris, a 29-year-old social entrepreneur who was inspired by her spunky 88-year-old grandmother. In addition to the cafe and the public toilets, Harris installed a roof-top garden built on the second floor.

The café was staffed by women, mostly over 60. They volunteered one shift a week and were promised a small share of the profits after three months. The idea was to stave off the social isolation too common among older people by bringing them into a place that valued their skills. As Helena Drakakis wrote in *The Guardian*, "Women who are made to feel they are on the scrapheap suddenly have purpose."

Comfort was on the menu and in the way the place was run. Reasonable prices attracted customers in search of affordable food, young mothers needing a place where babies and small children were welcomed, and people who sought a place to relax and chat.

In March 2015 a long-simmering dispute between the café and the non-profit renting them the space came to a head. The café closed its doors and may never re-open.

The restaurant's short life does not make it a failure. NANA Comfort Food Café provided a social-enterprise model that brightened a lot of lives. The older women who cooked the food and waited on the customers knew they were valued.

Read more:
- "Nana Café Embraces the Talents of Grandmothers"— http://goo.gl/FuPU32
- "NANA: A Café for Nanas, Run by Nanas, Seeks Crowd-Funding"— http://goo.gl/0fPx4H
- "A Granny-Run Café Housed in a Former Toilet Has Been Forced to Close"— https://goo.gl/2hhUwr

Part 4 - Never Too Old

The autumn of our years is a richly productive time. Dreams have no expiry date. We can use whatever talents we have right up until our last breath.

She Circumnavigated the Globe Solo

The oldest woman to make a solo, unassisted, non-stop circumnavigation of the globe sailed into the Inner Harbour of Victoria, B.C. on July 8, 2013. She was 70 years old.

Jeanne Socrates, a retired math teacher from the UK, had tried twice before. In 2009 she got as far as Cape Horn, where she had to stop three months for repairs. In 2011 her boat was damaged in a storm off the southern tip of South America. From there she continued to the Falklands, South Africa, Tasmania, Tahiti and Hawaii. She rounded the Five Great Capes of the Southern Ocean (Cape Horn, Cape of Good Hope, Cape Leeuwin, SE Cape of Tasmania, SW Cape of New Zealand) before sailing into the Strait of Juan de Fuca on August 1, 2012.

Determined to sail non-stop around the world, she set out from Victoria, B.C., in October 2012. She peppered her blog with a wealth of information about sailing, ocean research and scientific discoveries.

Socrates's sailing career began with her husband in her late 40s. They commissioned the first *Nereida* in 1997 and sailed it from the UK across the Atlantic. When cancer took her husband in 2008, she embarked on a solo sailing career.

That led not only to circumnavigating the globe but also to a string of medals, such as the Ocean Cruising Club's Special Award and the Cruising Club of America's Blue Water Medal. Neither the death of her husband and sailing partner, nor her own advancing age, deterred her from continually setting new goals.

Dreams do not have an expiry date, as Socrates demonstrates every time she steps onto the *Nereida* and sails solo toward open sea.

Read more:
- Jeanne Socrates's website — http://www.svnereida.com/
- "Solo Sailor Returns to Victoria after Global Journey; Oldest Woman to Accomplish Feat"— http://goo.gl/rCo9Jc
- "Jeanne Socrates Completes Solo, Non-Stop Circumnavigation"— http://goo.gl/2bhPk6

Immigrant Custodian Graduates from Columbia University

When Gac Filipaj received a classics degree, with honors, from Columbia University, he may have been 2012's most famous graduating student. The 52-year-old immigrant had earned his degree in 12 years, while working afternoons and evenings as a custodian at the university.

Filipaj fled war-torn Yugoslavia in 1992. He spoke little English, but his language tutor recognized his intelligence and suggested he find a job at Columbia, where employees can take tuition-free courses.

That was likely the best advice anyone in his new country gave Filipaj. The first courses he took were to improve his English. Then he tackled the core curriculum. Finally he moved on to the classics.

Twelve years of morning classes, shift work, commuting, and late-night studying later, Filipaj fulfilled his goal of graduating from one of the best universities in the world. Justifiably proud of his accomplishments, he hoped other older students would look at him and be encouraged to pursue education at any age.

Filipaj was confident he was not too old, inexperienced or unskilled to reach for the brass ring. He showed that dogged persistence can pay off, at any age.

Read more:

- "Custodian to Graduate from Columbia University after 19 Years"— http://goo.gl/ALhmO2
- "Ivy League Janitor: 'I'm Still Wearing the Gown'"— http://goo.gl/5zSu7Y
- "New Grad Notes 202: Gac Filipaj"— https://goo.gl/Y0HRCO

Record-setting Gymnast at 86

In April 2012 Johanna Quaas set a Guinness World Record as the world's oldest gymnast. Not bad for a woman who was nearing her 87th birthday.

Videos made while she was in her 80s show how strong, flexible and skilled the German-born gymnast still was. Interviewed for the Guinness World Record video, she explained she had always been athletic. When she became a teacher, she chose physical education for her area of concentration. In her late 50s she began competing.

Quaas was a strong contestant. When she was officially declared the oldest woman gymnast, the octogenarian became an Internet sensation. Millions watched her videos, studying her to see if they could figure out the secrets to her long years of athletic prowess. For Quaas there was no secret, just decades of working hard at something she loved.

Some people watching her perform in her 80s no doubt considered her "cute" in the patronizing way older women find themselves being called "young lady" or "sweetheart" by people a quarter their age. They needed to look again. Well into her 80s she could still perform feats most people cannot do in their twenties.

Quaas, still competing at the age of 89, is an inspiration for more than gymnastics. At a time when lack of exercise and poor diet are putting toddlers and teens at risk for heart disease and diabetes, Johanna Quaas stands out as a model for active living and healthy aging.

Read more:
- Guinness World Record Holders: Johanna Quaas, Oldest Gymnast — http://goo.gl/JLuWBB
- Guinness World Record video — https://youtu.be/RLeoreilVp0
- "Johanna Quaas, 89, the World's Oldest Active Gymnast, to Be Honored in Oklahoma City"— http://goo.gl/s62rIC

Sister Madonna Buder, Octogenarian Runner

Sister Madonna Buder keeps breaking records. In September 2012 the 82-year-old was in Penticton, at the south end of British Columbia's Lake Okanagan, prepared to make history. She managed that handily, as the first over-80 woman to complete the Ironman Canada, with a time of 16:32:00.

She did not stop to rest. That same October the Iron Nun was in Hawaii to compete in the Ironman there. She swam 2.4 miles in 2:01:50 and cycled 90 out of the required 112 miles before ending her bid to complete yet another major competition.

Undeterred, she continued training and two years later was back in Kailua to attempt to become the oldest person to ever complete a championship Ironman race. This time she did the swim in 2:18 and completed 74.7 miles of cycling before dropping out.

Sister Madonna started her running career in 1978. In 1982 she ran her first triathlon. Three years later, at 55, she competed in her first Ironman. By the time her book, *The Grace to Race: The Wisdom and Inspiration of the 80-Year-Old World Champion Triathlete Known as the Iron Nun,* was published she had run more than 340 triathlons.

She continued to compete. In July 2014 she was inducted into the USA Triathlon Hall of Fame, as part of the Class of 2013. In 2015 she was named the Ironman All World Athlete Champion for her age group.

As to when she will stop competing, she leaves that in God's hands. Until she hears the message, she will keep going, spreading what she considers the one common world language: love.

Some people pray on their knees. Sister Madonna prays as she cycles, swims and runs. As she moves, she repeats her mantra, "Praise the Lord. Bless His holy name."

Sister Madonna Buder inspires us to use whatever talents we possess, for as long as we have breath.

Read more:
- "Sister Madonna Named Ironman All World Athlete Champion"— http://goo.gl/YiUajA
- "The Ironwoman: Sister Madonna Buder"— http://goo.gl/5vKKNU

How Old Is Too Old?

For James Arruda Henry, the answer to "How old is too old?" was: "Never." He was 96 years old when he learned to read. Once he acquired literacy, he hand-wrote his autobiography, *In a Fisherman's Language*.

He might have gone to his grave unable to read and write, but he heard about George Dawson, who learned to read at the age of 98 and then co-authored his autobiography, *Life Is So Good*.

Henry was inspired. He started practicing his signature. Then he went on to a more challenging task, penning his autobiography. He had plenty of stories to tell. He had captained a lobster boat, been a boxer, and served in the National Guard. He had married, raised a family, and welcomed grandchildren.

All that time, he hid a secret that shamed him. He could not read or write. When he moved into an assisted-living residence in Mystic, Connecticut, he decided it was time to learn.

Mark Hogan, a retired English teacher, became his tutor. At first the volunteer had no idea at he was mentoring a budding author. His star student gradually moved from grasping the fundamentals of reading and writing to using what he learned to record his tales.

When he became a published author, his eyes shone with pride. Henry had only one opportunity to visit a classroom and inspire the third-grade students to be excited about literacy. He was too frail for other school visits and died on January 6, 2013.

His legacy lives on in his book, which is available in paperback and Kindle editions, and in the website his family maintains. He died a happy man, having accomplished the secret dream he had harbored so many years.

Read more:
- *In a Fisherman's Language* website — http://fishermanslanguage.com/
- "Acclaimed Stonington Author Jim Henry Dies at 99"— http://goo.gl/ABwzRL
- "A Legacy of Literacy 'In a Fisherman's Language'"— http://goo.gl/TgeFgu

Old People in Chairs

One of the quirkiest demonstrations of the capacities of older people is a performance art piece. Angie Hiesl's *x-times people chair*, has been mounted in Germany, Amsterdam, Brazil, Columbia, Peru and Montreal.

The German artist attaches white chairs five meters above the ground and asks volunteers to sit on them for an hour and do whatever they want to do. Only people 60 and older need apply.

x-times people chair celebrated its 10th anniversary in 2005. In 2012 it opened in Montreal. The first night was rained out but not before the seniors had mounted their chairs. They all had seat belts while they were in the chairs, but they had no safety harnesses as they climbed or descended the ladders that took them there.

Pat Donnelly, who wrote about the opening, was worried about their safety. She need not have been. If they suffered from acrophobia, they would never have made the climb. If they were wobbly on a ladder, they would have stayed on the ground.

No, these seniors were quite all right, thank you very much. They read newspapers, knitted, meditated or whatever else gave them pleasure during their hour on the high chairs.

People watching from below were compelled to re-examine some of their internalized stereotypes about aging and competency.

Read more:

- *x-times people chair* — http://goo.gl/2i35oQ
- "FTA's First Outdoor High Chair Show Rained Out"— http://goo.gl/Edm16v
- "X-Times People Chair: Angie Hiesl"— http://goo.gl/WufqKw

The WWII Vet Who Played Hooky

He pinned on his medals, pulled on a raincoat, and headed out the door of The Pines nursing home in Hove, East Sussex. Nothing was going to keep Bernard Jordan from attending the 2014 D-Day commemorations in Normandy.

The BBC reported that nursing home staff had tried to secure a place for him on a tour organized by the Royal British Legion. Unfortunately, the tour was fully booked. Rather than miss the ceremonies, Jordan took matters into his own hands. With a coat covering his medals, he set out on an adventure.

He overlooked one small thing. He did not tell staff in the nursing home he was not planning to come back from his daily jaunt. When he failed to return, they sent the police on a hunt.

The officials discovered he had taken the train to Portsmouth, where he connected with veterans on their way to France. One of them called the nursing home so they could stop worrying about the independent senior.

The 89-year-old veteran was a hit with everyone he met. He made it to the ceremonies and then took the overnight ferry back home. His cheerful personality won the hearts of the staff of Brittany Ferries, who offered him "free travel to the Normandy beaches for the rest of his life."

The story quickly went viral, a testament to the intrepid Bernard Jordan but also a reminder of the stereotypes about aging. D-Day was important to Jordan. He was fit enough to make the trip. His wife was not worried, and, after all, a nursing home is a residence, not a prison. Staff members were justly concerned, but Jordan knew if he announced his intention they would try to stop him.

He had no regrets when he returned home. In fact, he announced plans to go again the next year.

His plan to return to Normandy in 2015 ended when he died in January of that year. But before death came to claim him, he had a fabulous adventure, became a media darling and taught people a lesson.

Age does not define us. Our attitude toward life does.

Read more:
- "D-Day: Hove Veteran Disappears for Normandy Trip"— http://goo.gl/LoDPud

- "D-Day Veteran, 89, Who Ran off to France for Anniversary: 'I'd do it again'"— http://goo.gl/4Ee2zv
- "D-Day Veteran 'Escapee' Bernard Jordan Dies Aged 90"— http://goo.gl/r50NVk

Record-breaking Track Star in her 90s

Fascinated by a five-foot, 93-year-old athlete with 23 world records in track and field, Bruce Grierson set out to find out *What Makes Olga Run?* He wanted to know everything about her—her diet and sleep habits, her personality traits, and what drives her. What he learned changed his life.

Born in 1919, Olga Kotelko grew up in a farming family in Saskatchewan. She was always physically active, as a child and throughout her teaching years. After she retired at 65, she joined a slo-pitch team. At 77 she began her career in track and field.

Until she died of a brain hemorrhage at the age of 95, she kept up a year-around regimen of workouts and swimming so she could be in top form for the track-and-field season. Her 37 world records in track and field events were a fraction of the over 700 gold medals she acquired in her last two decades.

Kotelko's athletic prowess and indomitable spirit attracted researchers with the same question Grierson had: How did she stay vigorous well into her 90s? What they learned confirmed the lessons of healthy aging found in active seniors around the world. She paid attention to her body's needs, ate a high quality diet and kept fit with daily exercise. She was sociable and enjoyed the company of family, friends and fellow athletes.

Just as notable was her upbeat attitude. Kotelko walked in sunshine of her own making. When asked for advice on healthy aging, she encouraged people to follow their dreams, at any age.

Kotelko was a remarkable example of the power of the mind, as well as the role of maintaining a healthy lifestyle. In spring 2014 Kotelko's own book was released. *Olga: The OK Way to a Healthy, Happy Life* promised "to start you on the path to fitness and longevity."

It would be hard to imagine a better role model. Olga Kotelko called herself "plain Jane". She was anything but ordinary.

Read more:
- Olga Kotelko website — http://www.olgakotelko.com/
- "What Makes Olga Run?" video — https://youtu.be/k9VO8N97Vjw

The Turbaned Tornado

Other 100-year-olds may have Facebook pages, but no other centenarians have completed a marathon in 8 hours, 25 minutes and 18 seconds. That is what Fauja Singh did in October 2011, when he achieved his goal of completing the Toronto marathon.

Singh's Facebook page indicates he was a farmer. After his wife died in 1992, he moved to London, England, to live with his son. To fight boredom and the deterioration that can come from a sedentary life, he took up running.

Running became his passion. At 89 he completed the London Marathon in 6 hours and 54 minutes, a new world record. He bested that record at 92, when he crossed the finish line at the Toronto Waterfront Marathon in 5 hours and 40 minutes. He was 101 when he participated in the Olympic torch relay. Shortly before his 102nd birthday he completed a 10-kilometer run at the Hong Kong marathon, coming in with a time of one hour, 32 minutes and 28 seconds.

Hong Kong was his last competition but not the end of his running. Singh continues to fuel his athleticism with a vegetarian diet. He avoids fried foods and grains and drinks only water and tea with ginger. A devout Sikh, he competes to raise funds for charities.

Kushwant Singh documented his life and rise to fame in a biography, using Fauja Singh's nickname, *Turbaned Tornado*, as the title.

The elderly runner once told Guardian reporter Nosheen Iqbal, "Why worry about these small, small things? I don't stress. You never hear of anyone dying of happiness."

As Singh runs his 10 to 15 kilometers a day — "you have to keep your engine going" — he is an inspiring example of taking whatever lemons life gives us and turning them into lemonade.

Read more:
- "Fauja Singh Has Done It!"— http://goo.gl/mnas0A
- "The Secret of the World's Oldest Marathon Runner"— http://goo.gl/uZonww
- "World's Oldest Marathon Man, 102, Can't Imagine Life without Running Shoes"— http://goo.gl/9BLXY0

Never Too Old to Chase Your Dreams

At 64, and after four earlier attempts, Diana Nyad finally achieved her dream of swimming non-stop and unassisted from Cuba to southern Florida. On September 2, 2013, after swimming 53 hours and 110 miles, through waters that were home to sharks and jellyfish, the exhausted swimmer staggered ashore in Key West.

Nyad had made her first attempt in 1978, but this route was particularly hazardous. Swimming in high seas in a steel shark cage, she was pushed off course and ended the swim after 76 miles.

When she turned 60, she was overcome by the sense of malaise that can come with an awareness of how fleeting life is. For her, the cure was to throw everything into achieving her dream.

In July 2010 she began training for another attempt. In August 2011 she set out again, this time without a shark cage but with electronic "Shark Shields". After 29 hours, an asthma flare-up forced her to abandon the attempt.

In September 2011 she swam 41 hours before jellyfish and Portuguese man-of-war stings forced her to call it quits. She swam even further on her fourth attempt, in August 2012, but storms and jellyfish stings made her give up short of her goal.

Then on August 31, 2013, she began her fifth attempt. This time she wore a full bodysuit, face mask, gloves and booties to protect her from jellyfish stings. On September 2, after 53 hours in the water, she emerged victorious.

Nyad never gave up on her dream, in spite of reaching an age most people consider too old for any kind of athletic achievement. She had a supportive team, but the dream, the swimming, the strength and the inner willpower were all hers.

Between Nyad's first and last attempts, 35 years passed. That is a long time to hang onto a dream, and to tackle it again after age 60 is extraordinary. As she writes articles and books and gives frequent lectures, she delivers these messages: Hard work, clear goals and determination cut through barriers. Age is not a good excuse for giving up. Failure is just a steppingstone.

Read more:

- "'Never, ever give up': Diana Nyad Completes Historic Cuba-to-Florida Swim"— http://goo.gl/w1NoMY

Part 5 - Feisty Aging

Concrete walls rose around her, but Edith Macefield refused to sell, even when the developers offered her a million dollars. We cannot hold back the years. We can determine how to live them well.

Make No Small Plans

The dream of saying goodbye to jobs and fixed addresses sometimes seduces adventurous people to sell their worldly goods and take to the road. Most people just talk about doing it. Joei Carlton Hossack took the plunge.

She and her husband Paul were living in Toronto when the travel bug bit them so badly they sold their home, furniture, boat and vehicles. He left behind a high-profile job with Merrill Lynch. She closed her wool shop. In 1989 they went to England, bought a motorhome and traveled for the next two and a half years.

Anyone who makes such a dramatic shift can expect both skepticism and envy from their friends. A couple not yet in their fifties will likely be suspected of having completely given up all pretense of rational thought.

The Hossacks never looked back. From the U.K. they went on to Europe, Africa and North America. They were in northern Germany when, in

1992, Paul was out jogging. The 52-year-old had a heart attack and died. Joei kept on traveling.

Now 71, she is still traveling. She is a prolific writer, whose books include memoirs, travel adventures, and what she calls "Mini Reads". She publishes articles about her adventures and is frequently the subject of media stories. She is a popular speaker and workshop leader, teaching classes in memoir and travel writing.

It takes a lot of gumption to travel solo for more than 20 years and to build a life and make a living out of a spirit of adventure. Joei Carlton Hossack has done it.

Hossack is one of those strong lamps who light the dark path between dream and reality. She did not set aside her dream because she thought she would fail, was afraid to jeopardize her pension or was too old to start. She did not wait until some magical date when all the stars would align. She was not afraid to be alone. When Joseph Campbell advised people to follow their bliss, he was probably thinking about people like Joei Carlton Hossack.

Read more:

- Joei Carlton's website — http://joeicarlton.com/

Aging With Zest

Whatever stereotypes you might have about aging would be shattered by the talented actors, storytellers, and singers at Stagebridge. The Oakland-based company is America's longest-running senior theatre troupe. Cast members come from varied backgrounds, taking the stage when retirement allows them time to pursue passions.

I got to know Stagebridge firsthand when they advertised for a storytelling director. They were looking for someone with experience in three areas: storytelling, education and community development. I had all three.

I called the number on the ad and said, "I think you're looking for me" (a story that netted me third place in the Impowerage writing contest). I managed to persuade Stagebridge they were, indeed, searching for what I had to offer and spent the next fifteen months being regularly blown away by the talent of people who ranged from their mid-50s to their 90s.

At the time I went to work for Stagebridge, I was well into my 50s. An interesting but challenging marriage had left my spirits in tatters, and I hadn't a clue how I was going to keep a roof over my head as I edged toward crone status. What these amazing people taught me was resilience. Some were financially stable. Others were struggling. Some were healthy. Others were dealing with chronic diseases, cancer, arthritis, and other debilitating conditions.

What they had in common was zest for life. They were the best kind of chosen family, the kind that asks how you are doing, empathizes with your problems, and then says, "Right. Sorry to hear that. I'll bring dinner around. But right now, the show must go on."

And go on it did, through improv, plays, comedy, dance, and storytelling. They had creativity to their fingertips and determination in every bone. They gave me hope that the last chapter of my life would be wild and wonderful, that I had enough bounce in me to get past my current difficulties, and that I still had time to add my voice to the chorus.

What they taught me about aging with zest stays with me today. We cannot hold back the years. We can choose to live vibrant, active lives.

Read more:
- Stagebridge website — http://stagebridge.org/
- "Curtain Call – Senior Theater's Dramatic Growth"— http://goo.gl/FWdI7i
- "Seniors Reaching Out"— http://goo.gl/1irTqj

Edythe Kirchmaier's Longevity Secrets

When Edythe Kirchmaier renewed her driver's license on January 22, 2008, she was given the normal five-year extension. That is rare for someone born in 1908, but Kirchmaier is lively, vibrant and still committed to volunteer work for her favorite charity, Direct Relief, where she shows up every week to hand write thank-you letters to donors.

For her 95th birthday, Kirchmaier's children gave her the first computer she had ever owned. Along with it came a digital camera and a printer. A lot of older people shy away from new technology. Kirchmaier embraced it.

When she went to sign up for Facebook she ran into a glitch. The site would not recognize a birthdate 100 years in the past. Once Facebook engineers fixed the problem, she was up and running and quickly acquired a loyal following.

Kirchmaier's age brings her media attention, but it is her irrepressible good spirits and her community spirit that inspire her fans.

Although centenarians are becoming increasingly common, they are still something of an anomaly. That gives us an unprecedented opportunity to rethink aging and to tap into the experience and knowledge people acquire over the decades.

Read more:
- "Ellen DeGeneres to Edythe: What's Your Secret?"— http://goo.gl/9jYpSi
- "Edythe Kirchmaier, Facebook's Oldest User, Shares Her Beautiful Wisdom"— http://goo.gl/FV6Dfe
- "Say Happy Birthday to Facebook's Oldest User"— http://goo.gl/22AdgJ

They Lift What's Dragging

D ragon boating demands commitment, time and a willingness to cooperate. Although primarily a younger person's sport, in Kelowna, B.C., it also attracts seniors.

The sport dates back two millennia in China. Oared longboats designed for military operations were rowed by highly trained squadrons, 30 men to each boat. The need for training led to boat racing.

The modern sport began in Hong Kong in 1976, as a means of encouraging tourism. It expanded into Asia, Europe and Canada over the next decade.

During the months before competition begins in Kelowna, we can look out our window and watch teams training for strength, speed, endurance and strategy. One boat in particular always grabs our attention. It is rowed by a club called "Lift What's Draggin". They are the only senior team in Kelowna and one of only a handful in the province. Add all their ages together, divide by the number of team members, and the average would be somewhere in the 60s.

They work hard at their training on Lake Okanagan. Each member is important to the whole. If one is missing, the empty space affects balance and speed. Commitment is essential. Only by pulling together can they achieve a respectable time during competitions.

When we see them working together to move a boat swiftly through the water, we do not see age in their movements. We see a team of people who have awakened their inner dragons. They remind us that if we lift what's dragging in our bodies and our spirits, we will pull the dragon boats of our lives to a stronger finish.

Read more:
- "Dragon Boat – History and Culture"— http://www.idbf.org/about_history.php
- Kelowna Dragon Boat Club website — https://goo.gl/s54C5h

Kelowna's Dance Hall Legend

The OK Corral in Kelowna, B.C., is not the same without the hero of its dance floor, Arnie Davis. Fortunately, young filmmaker Chelsea McEvoy met the aging dancer before he took off his dancing boots for the last time. She knew his was a story worth telling.

For twenty years the talented dancer twirled women around the floor night after night. He told McEvoy the secret to attracting girls was to learn how to dance. He never ran out of partners.

Davis's dancing years started early, when his sisters needed a partner so they could practice their moves. They wore out the old gramophone but wanted to keep dancing. One of them would hand spin the records.

Arnie Davis put away his dancing shoes during his 35-year marriage. When divorce left him free to dance again, he became a regular at the OK Corral, in the town he had come to call home. Young women and old, he danced with them all. When his health became precarious, McEvoy was there to record his last dance in the pub where he had found community.

McEvoy's questions brought out Arnie's memories and the homespun wisdom of a man who learned how to give and receive joy in spite of any hard balls life threw his way. When CBC interviewed McEvoy about the documentary on November 22, 2013, Arnie was in hospice, his attitude still sunny as he edged closer to death.

On July 22, 2014, lung cancer ended the dancer's life but not the place he held in the memories of those who came to mourn him. They gathered to honor the legacy of a man who danced his way into their hearts.

Read more:
- "Arnie: a Local Legend" (documentary) — https://youtu.be/LSUQcaJ0zkQ
- "Arnie's Last Dance Will Never End"— http://goo.gl/fqehUx
- "One Last Two-Step for 79-Year-Old Cowboy"— http://goo.gl/6hmSkP

Sometimes We Are Incredibly Brave

The 75-year-old British Columbia woman did not feel right about kicking cougars, but the wild cats were attacking her dog. Jacqui Simenson was walking her two Shih Tzus, Teddy and Bear, along a Sayward beach when two cougars ran out of a shack. One snatched Bear. That was a mistake on the cougar's part. Simenson swung into action.

CTV News interviewed Simenson, whose quick reaction saved the dog. She told them when the cougar let go of Bear, she scooped up the dogs and ran to a nearby log sort for help. One of the workers took her home. Her husband was proud of the way her mothering instinct kicked in, even though it overpowered her need for personal safety.

Cpl. Milo Ramsey of the Sayward RCMP reluctantly shot the young cougars. He had never encountered cougars before and had an affinity for wildlife. However, because the area was popular for walkers and boaters, he felt the risk to humans was high. Simenson also felt badly about the cougars' being shot and had no intention of taking on another.

Simenson acted out of instinct and saved her pets. People who heard of her dog rescue were reminded of an important lesson. Sometimes when things are at their worst, we are braver and smarter than we imagine we will be, at any age.

Read more:
- "Feisty Senior Saves Pet Dog from Hungry Cougars"— http://goo.gl/Qysnjl
- "Vancouver Island Senior Fights Off Cougars Attacking Dog"— http://goo.gl/zm0OzU

Scooter Gran a Hit with Skateboarders

She became an icon in Perth, Scotland and a virtual hit on the Internet. Barbel Roerig, a 74-year-old retired architectural technician, found herself dubbed "Scooter Gran".

Roerig actually started using the scooter in her mid-sixties, after she saw Oslo airport staff carrying things on one. She gave it a try and never stopped. The scooter gave her safe transportation, kept her active and healthy, and took her places the bus did not. It was easy on her knees and could carry her bags as she scooted around on her errands. Shops grew accustomed to seeing her and would allow her to bring her scooter inside.

She had been scootering nearly a decade when she became an international darling. One camera-wearing skateboarder posted a video of her on YouTube. He and his pals had stopped to meet the German-born Roerig. The video of the interaction went viral.

Medical researchers at Glasgow Caledonian University were curious to know if Roerig's mode of transportation could ease joint problems in seniors. They were surprised to learn scootering reduced load leg by as much as 67 percent.

When mechanical problems with her trusty scooter took 74-year-old Scooter Gran off the road in 2013, the *Daily Record* paired her with Micro Scooters UK and stunt rider Toren Jarritt. After three hours of testing different models, Roerig settled on the Micro White scooter. It met her exacting standards.

Barbel Roerig just might create a whole new global market for scooters. As earth-friendly transport for active seniors, they have a lot to offer.

Read more:
- "Perth 'Scooter Gran' Becomes Internet Hit"— http://goo.gl/DeSCUv
- "Scientists Prove Web Sensation Gran's Scooter Can Help OAP's Beat Leg Aches and Pains"— http://goo.gl/L3d0UT
- "Scooter Granny – the Ultimate Test"— http://goo.gl/9dJgG5

A Little Old Woman
Who Said NO to Power

Edith Macefield was happy in the old farmhouse and wanted to live there until she died. As Seattle's Ballard neighborhood densified around her, she hung on.

Her blue-collar neighborhood became upscale. Developers offered her $1 million to sell her home. Macefield stayed put. When concrete walls were poured within inches of her home, she turned up the television and tuned out the noise.

Around the world she became a symbol of gritty determination. She grew old and frail but still clung to her independence and her house.

Then Barry Martin came into her life. He had been hired as senior superintendent on the construction project towering around her home.

The younger man quickly realized there was no way he could persuade Macefield to move out of the path of development. In spite of her irascibility, he brought her food, took her to the doctor, and spent hours talking with her. She was no sweet, docile old lady and was often short tempered with the man who was doing so much for her.

He hung in there anyway. The unlikely pals proved to have a lot in common. Both were stubborn and opinionated. They were bright and curious. They loved a good argument. Martin stuck by her until she died of pancreatic cancer at the age of 86. She left her house to him.

Martin wrote a book about Macefield after she died. He called it *Under One Roof: Lessons I Learned from a Tough Old Woman in a Little Old House*. If the story sounds familiar but you never heard of Edith Macefield, you may be thinking of a story with a very similar theme, the Disney/Pixar movie, *Up*.

Sometimes it is hard to stay the course in the face of powerful forces. Edith Macefield did. Years after her death people were still tying balloons to her fence, like those in the movie. Inside the balloons were messages about an old woman who said "No!" to power, from people who felt a little more courageous because of her.

Read more:
- "Ballard Woman Held her Ground as Change Closed in around Her"— http://goo.gl/88xOQJ
- "Sale Pending on Edith Macefield 'Up' House in Ballard"— http://goo.gl/j1YD3Y
- "Ballard's Macefield House: A Lot of Symbolism for a Little House"— http://goo.gl/1zFWg1

The Pensioner Who Scared the Thieves

Ann Timson was in her 70s when she used her handbag to stop six, sledge hammer-wielding robbers.

The scene in Spring Boroughs, Northampton startled everyone who heard about it. The thieves arrived on three scooters and began smashing the windows of a jewelry store and pulling out watches, rings and necklaces.

This was not some midnight heist. They attacked the store in broad daylight, while people went on about their business. In fact, someone stood there videotaping the whole thing.

Suddenly red-coated Ann Timson came on the run. She swung her handbag and began bashing the thieves. This is where the camera-toting bystander came in handy, recording the pensioner as she swung away, without a thought for her own safety.

The gang gave up and fled, but one guy fell off his scooter. Finally a passerby came forward and helped Timson. The two of them detained the robber until police came. No one was hurt, and the miscreants were rounded up.

In her statement to the Northamptonshire Police, Ann Timson said she thought one of the kids was being beaten. She ran over to help. Her comments on the incident:

A lot were standing there filming or taking photos and I wonder whether more people didn't intervene because they thought the raid was being mocked up.

In the cold light of day, I know I put myself in danger. But I probably would do the same again.

My red coat has now been packed away for the winter and my red hair is being dyed green. And my black shopping bag is having a rest today, to give it time to recover from its bruises!

Ann Timson showed gumption. The world could use a lot more people like her.

Read more:
- "'Supergran' Who Clobbered Robbers Angry That Others Watched"— http://goo.gl/eqkOP1
- "Pensioner Prevented Jewellery Raid 'through misunderstanding'"— http://goo.gl/OTTUsy
- "'Super Granny' Who Clobbered Robbers: 'I'm not a hero"— http://goo.gl/L04NkQ

Zip Lining at 100, BASE Jumping at 102

Dorothy Custer, born in 1911, may have been the world's oldest amateur comedian when she died. She had been at it from the age of five, when she discovered how much she enjoyed being in the limelight with family, friends and gatherings. She never looked back. Nearly a hundred years later, the Twin Falls, Idaho, centenarian was still popular, delivering hilarious lines with aplomb.

Jay Leno learned about her and invited her to appear on his show in June 2011. She cracked jokes, played the harmonica and stole audience hearts. Early in the interview, she told Leno the wind was blowing her skirt up when she visited Universal Studios the day before. She was hanging onto her hat when a young fellow told her she'd better let go of the hat and pull her dress down because, "You're showing everything you got."

She told him, "I don't care. What they see down there is 100 years old. This is a brand-new hat."

Popular with media in her hometown, Custer charmed them by going zip lining for her 100th birthday, BASE jumping on her 102nd, and riding an elephant for the first time when she was 102. She celebrated turning 103 in a hot air balloon high over Park City, Utah. Had she reached her 104th birthday in May 2015, she would have tackled yet another adventure, but she died in April.

An impish spirit kept Custer going, along with the healthy diet, regular exercise and social connections that characterize so many who reach advanced age.

Dorothy Custer set the bar high for happy aging. Life is a wild ride. She laughed all the way.

Read more:
- "Watch Video of Dorothy Custer on Tonight Show with Jay Leno"— http://goo.gl/MYHAp5
- "102-Year-Old Celeb Dorothy Custer BASE Jumps from Idaho Bridge"— http://goo.gl/pLRA5I
- "Dorothy Custer Turns 103"— https://youtu.be/cMFm9fk-DDc

First U.S. Plastics Ban Due to Octogenarian

When her 8-year-old grandson told her about the huge plastic gyres polluting our oceans, 82-year-old Jean Hill started digging into the environmental issues at stake. She was appalled to learn about the impact on aquifers and wildlife, how long plastic takes to degrade, how much fossil fuel is required to manufacture it, and the effects on waterways and oceans.

Hill had been campaigning for social justice since she was a 16-year-old trying to start a union in the factory where she had a summer job. She was the right person to galvanize supporters around the issue. When *Concord Conserves* asked her if recycling would resolve her concern, she reminded them the issue was far larger. Only reducing our use of plastics would alleviate it.

The International Bottled Water Association threatened legal action if Concord enacted a bylaw. Critics claimed their freedom of choice was being unfairly impinged on. Businesses worried about the financial impact they would bear.

Nothing stopped Hill's pursuit of her goal. Thanks to her doggedness and the support of other activists, her historic town of Concord, Massachusetts, rang in the new year of 2013 with a ban on the sale of plastic water bottles.

Jean Hill was the driving force behind the first plastic-bottle ban in America. She was an example to her grandson and an inspiration to anyone who wonders if one small voice can make a difference.

Read more:
- "What We Do: An Interview with Jean Hill"— http://goo.gl/lI0w59
- "84-Year-Old Grandmother's Crusade to Ban Bottled Water"— http://goo.gl/47Y9bq
- "Concord's Jean Hill and Jill Appel Honored by EPA"— http://goo.gl/WTa3lL

Rockin' Granny

One of the hottest DJs on the rock scene was nearly seventy when she began her career.

Ruth Flowers dazzled young audiences in some of the most popular nightspots in Europe. Known as Mamy Rock, she fell in love with dance music and the energy of the club atmosphere when her grandson took her to a London nightclub to celebrate his birthday. She almost did not get in because she did not fit the demographic.

She knew that night she wanted to be a DJ. She was a vibrant, 69-year-old widow with plenty of determination. Her grandson was skeptical, but she was not just daydreaming. On her website she wrote that an acquaintance introduced her to Aurelien Simon, a young French producer who heard her story and encouraged her to go for it.

With Simon's help, she learned the skills needed for DJing, developed an image, and debuted at a celebration during the 2009 Cannes Film Festival.

From that point on she wowed audiences across Europe, the U.S., Australia and Asia. With her trademark sunglasses, spiky hair and bling, Flowers looked the part, except for the signs of her years on the planet. White hair and wrinkles did not bother her young fans, who loved the music she mixed and cheered whenever she appeared.

She was a combination of style, sass, and grandmotherly approachability. Her popularity soared. She was in her element.

On May 27, 2014, the effervescent, 82-year-old Mamy Rock died. Her website remains live, as a tribute to the woman who inspired so many.

Rest in peace, Mamy Rock. You were a role model for feisty aging and for living with passion throughout life.

Read more:
- Mamy Rock website — http://www.mamyrock.com/
- "Mamy Rock: Silver-haired DJ Sensation"— http://goo.gl/isAEPI
- "82-Year-Old DJ Ruth Flowers 'Mamy Rock' Dead"— http://goo.gl/HdbRQt

World War II Vet Runs across the U.S.

Ernie Andrus set out on the run of his life. He started at the Pacific Ocean near San Diego in October 2013, two months after his 90th birthday. His plan was to keep running until he touched the Atlantic Ocean.

Andrus came late to long-distance running. He completed his first half marathon when he was 87, his second when he was 89. Just for fun he did four 200-mile relays in the year in between.

He had a goal in mind when he began his cross-country run: to earn enough money from sponsors to send the U.S.S. LST 325, a decommissioned naval ship, back to France in time for the 75th anniversary of the 1944 invasion of Normandy. The goal was important to the veteran but not as important as the run itself. He had read of other people doing cross-country runs for a cause. The idea intrigued him.

At a pace of three to ten miles a day, a cross-country run is incredibly long. The *Bronwood (Texas)*

Bulletin celebrated his arrival there on May 7, 2015. On June 18th he ran through Dallas.

His Facebook page tracks his progress on a daily basis. As of this writing he is still a long way from the Atlantic, but he will likely keep going until he reaches it.

It takes strength of character to keep going mile after mile, year after year, doggedly pursuing an elusive goal. Andrus has plenty of that. Whether or not he raises the millions needed to send that ship to France, or even whether or not he reaches the Atlantic, Ernie Andrus is a winner. His run is more about setting a personal goal than reaching the destination. He inspires people with every mile.

Read more:
- "Ernie Andrus Comes to Brownwood"— http://goo.gl/w7hsvu
- Ernie Andrus's website — http://coast2coastruns.com/
- "Vet Runs across U.S. in Honor of Unsung WWII Hero"— http://goo.gl/eziDnu

Part 6 - Parts of Me Still Work

Embrace your aging body and the years that brought you to this point. We are never too old to walk barefoot in the sand.

Taking on the Youth and Beauty Police

If you want to know "what it's really like to get old," drop by Time Goes By and the related blog, Elder Storytelling Place. Since 2005 the site has been maintained by writers who speak with candor and humor about the realities of aging.

For example, Jeanne Waite Follett's "Father Time Is My Peer" is written from the perspective of a woman who is healthy but does not take that for granted. Joanne Zimmerman's "Worried to Death" tackles the difficult subject of dying. William Weatherstone's poignant piece, "The Nursing Home", explores the ache that could be part of anyone's future: watching a loved one with Alzheimer's slowly deteriorate.

Movie lovers wanting to watch something other than lithe, young actors can check out Geezer Flicks and Elder Video. Another section suggests a handful of the Best Books on Aging.

Stories come from dozens of people, including a very articulate group of regular columnists. As

Ronni Bennett, the site's founder and former managing editor of CBSNews.com, told AARP (American Association of Retired People): "Ninety-eight percent of what is written about getting older is about disease, decline and disability. I'm trying to be an advocate for older people by taking on the youth and beauty police."

Check it out if you are old enough to feel the issues of aging in your bones – or if you look at age as a distant and fearsome land. Find companions here for the journey we all must make.

Read more:
- Time Goes By website — http://www.timegoesby.net/
- "Older, Wiser Bloggers"— http://goo.gl/AdeMji
- "Blogging through the Ages"— http://goo.gl/eUVBHZ

In Praise of the Aging Body

Alice Matzkin was 58 when she looked in the mirror and saw gravity pulling down every part of her body. Her husband was struggling with his own worries about aging. Instead of running from their fears, the two artists decided to explore them. Richard began sculpting naked old men. Alice painted nude elder women, ranging in age from 58 to 87.

The work they created through their focus on aging is extraordinary. In addition to a continually growing body of painting and sculpture, they produced a book, *The Art of Aging: Celebrating the Authentic Aging Self* and an inspiring documentary, *Women of Age: Portraits in Wisdom, Beauty and Strength.* Two of Alice's paintings are in the permanent collection of the National Art Gallery at the Smithsonian Institution.

Alice Matzkin is in her early 70s, Richard in his late 60s. When they speak in the videos linked from their website, their love for and acceptance of each other is palpable. How wise they have been to closely examine their own aging bodies and those of the men and women who have posed for them. What they have seen in their subjects and in each other are beauty and endurance rather than decay.

Their message is very different from the endless ads for products to hide wrinkles, cover grey hair, and perpetuate a myth of never-ending youthfulness. The Matzkins show the exquisite beauty in old faces, old bodies and old lovers. Their reverence for their elderly models pulls the plug on bottled-up fears of loss and replaces them with deep acceptance and joy.

Alice and Richard Matzkin are encouraging guides on the aging journey. One couple cannot overcome all of society's distaste for everything that surrounds aging and death. What they can do is inspire us to examine our own stereotypes and embrace our aging bodies and the years of accumulated experience that got us to this point.

Read more:
- Alice and Richard Matzkin website — http://matzkinstudio.com/
- "The Tender Beauty of Aging with Alice and Richard Matzkin"— http://goo.gl/n1ojwD
- "Conscious Aging through Art: Couple Finds Beauty and Peace in Aging"— http://goo.gl/3cWIB9

ElderSpirit Brings Depth to Aging

Our North American views on aging need a tuneup. Instead of defining seniors as an accumulation of losses and a drain on limited resources, we could be viewing our elders as entering a liberating time of inner growth that can benefit the broader society.

Since 1996 Drew Leder, a professor in the Philosophy Department at Loyola University Maryland, has called for a different model of aging. He envisions Elder Spirit Centers, communities and resource centers for older adults interested in spiritual growth.

One woman who understands that dream and, at the age of 71, set it in motion is Geraldine "Dene" Peterson. She had already spent a lifetime serving the poor, first as a Glenmary Sister, then, after age 35, outside the order. When she finally retired at 70, she collaborated with a few others to create the kind of retirement community she wanted to live in.

ElderSpirit, the first senior cohousing community in the U.S., lies near the Virginia Creeper Trail in Abingdon, Virginia. It is a mixed-income community where some residents own their own homes, while others rent. They come together to prepare shared meals, work in the gardens, volunteer for communal tasks and pursue common interests.

The spiritually diverse community is small. They live in a cluster of 16 rental units and 13 owner-occupied units. Since this is a cohousing community, not a care home, some residents do reach a time when they have to move to a place where they can receive assistance. When that time comes, the care committee swings into action to find the right home and maintain connection with the departing resident.

The warm, caring spirit of the founder permeates the community, which has become a model for healthy aging in place. People come from far away to study ElderSpirit.

Isolation and loneliness are thieves of emotional and physical health for many seniors. Those who choose to live in ElderSpirit remain vibrantly engaged, with each other, the nearby community, and their spiritual lives.

We were never meant to grow old alone, but it is a hard reality of modern life. We need more communities like ElderSpirit and Baba Yaga House.

Read more:
- ElderSpirit Community website — http://elderspirit.org/
- "Shared Meals, and Lives"— http://goo.gl/jAF7NG
- "Small Virginia Community Was Organized by Former Catholic Nuns"— http://goo.gl/3SVOAa

Healthy Aging in Baba Yaga House

Please give a standing ovation to the French government for providing four million euros to a group of aging feminists to build the Baba Yaga House. The government will likely recoup that investment in lower health-related costs as the women age.

Each of the 24 apartments is 40 square meters (just over 430 square feet). Residents are women aged sixty and older. Thérèse Clerc, the activist in her 80s who kickstarted the project, says her generation of women had large families and too little time in the work force to build up good pensions. By pooling their strengths and resources, they can age in place and in community. The self-managed home in the Parisian suburb of Montreuil allows them to retain their independence by supporting each other.

Residents not only live together and look after each other, they continue working on behalf of women's rights. They have set aside an 80 square meter space on the ground floor for an open university, where they can run courses and discussion groups, creative writing sessions, concerts and anything else that supports healthy aging. They also have a 20 square meter apartment for visitors. Should they need more onsite care in future, they can make that space available for visiting doctors and nurses.

The dream was decades from initial idea to reality. Clerc began thinking about her own aging when she was in her mid-60s. Visits to state-run seniors' residences convinced her she could not endure the regimented, controlled life they offered. So she and her group of close, feminist friends began lobbying for an alternative. They were ultimately successful, though Clerc was 85 by the time the women, in their 60s, 70s and 80s, moved into their six-story seniors' home.

Many are gazing into their personal crystal balls and watching the time approach when they may want to pool limited resources with those of friends. They want a dignified, affordable living situation, surrounded by people with whom they are compatible and know they can rely on.

California's Bay Area has seniors' homes organized around interests other than age. One, for example, is for activists, the other for performers (musicians, actors and dancers). Other options also exist, such as the Abbeyfield Houses, which can be found in countries around the world. Some are still in the thinking stage, such as Janet Torge's idea of Radical Resthomes, prompted by a story she produced for CBC.

The demand for more affordable housing ideas will increase in the coming decades. More options are needed that acknowledge people are not all alike just because they are old.

Read more:
- "The Babayagas' House, a Feminist Alternative to Old People's Homes, Opens in Paris"— http://goo.gl/opfIDc
- Radical Resthomes website — http://radicalresthomes.com/
- "Baba Yaga's House" (documentary) — http://goo.gl/iGnnha

Singing Tunes Our Brains

Anyone who enjoys belting out a song knows how good it feels. For those who still hear that voice from childhood saying, "Just mouth the words," storyteller Jay O'Callahan has this advice: "Sing in the key of free."

My partner, Robin Jarman, is a talented pianist much in demand these days to play what he calls "tunes of yesteryear" for older audiences. Whether people sing along, hum the tunes, tap out the beat or just listen, you can see memories playing across their faces. Often someone comes up to him after a performance and tells him a story one of his songs evoked.

In the past couple of years he has occasionally been asked to lead a singing group for Sing for Your Life, a program launched in Kelowna, B.C., by Nigel Brown. Brown's brother, Stuart, started the program in the UK and could see the impact on the elders who participated.

I went with Robin to one of the Silver Song Group sessions and was moved when a woman brought her mother. She quietly told Robin the older woman had dementia. Her participation might be limited. But within the growing muddle of her mother's thinking processes was an untouched file. In it were stored the songs of a lifetime. Tunes and words were intact. So was the joy on both women's faces, as they joined in with the familiar songs.

Researchers are discovering that singing leads to more than joy. Though that alone would be enough, it actually improves health. A study by George Mason University found that dementia patients in a care home increased their cognitive abilities after four months of singing classes. A similar study at the University of Helsinki showed improvements in mood, orientation and memory after ten weeks of singing. The results were still there six months later. Another study, by Canterbury Christ Church University in the UK, found the same effects.

Of course, the benefits are not limited to seniors. In 2000, researchers from Canterbury Christ Church University surveyed 84 members of a university college choral society. They reported such things as "benefits for well-being and relaxation, benefits for breathing and posture, social benefits, spiritual benefits, emotional benefits, and benefits for heart and immune system." A 2010 study by the

Beth Israel Deaconess Medical Center and Harvard Medical School showed speech improvements in people with conditions such as stuttering, Parkinson's disease, acquired brain lesions, and autism.

So if anyone tells you to just mouth the words or insists music is an unaffordable luxury in schools or care homes, point them to the research. Tell them to check out the links below and maybe even branch out and look at other studies. (There are more.) Then invite them to come with you to a sing-along. It just might improve their life, and yours.

Read more:
- Sing For Your Life Canada website — http://singforyourlife-canada.org/
- "Alzheimer's Patients' Brains Boosted by Belting out Sound of Music"— http://goo.gl/cym9Cb
- "Cognitive, Emotional, and Social Benefits of Regular Musical Activities in Early Dementia: Randomized Controlled Study"— http://goo.gl/4cZkyU
- "Does a 'Singing Together Group' Improve the Quality of Life of People with a Dementia and their Carers? A Pilot Evaluation Study"— http://dem.sagepub.com/content/12/2/157

Care Home Residents Are YouTube Stars

Residents of the Waverly Mansion in London, Ontario, are not settling for a boring stay in an assisted-living facility. With the urging of their recreation co-ordinator, Sarah Urquhart, the oldsters are becoming YouTube stars.

Urquhart had no idea her first production would be such a hit. Residents danced and lip-synched to Carly Rae Jepsen's "Call Me Maybe". Urquhart edited the video, uploaded it to YouTube and watched the hits roll in. It has been viewed over a million times.

Fired up by the success of the first video, the residents went on to do a Gangnam Style video, then the "Harlem Shake", Michael Jackson's "Thriller", and a version of the old-time favorite, "Singing in the Rain", that gives new meaning to "chin music".

All retirement homes have recreation programs, ranging from fitness to bridge. They generally happen within the walls of the facility or on scheduled outings. Urquhart has hit on an idea that allows elderly residents to engage with a broader community even if they are unable to leave the residence. With ageism a significant issue and threats of a "grey tsunami" creating even more schisms among generations, these videos may help shred some of the stereotyping of Old People as useless and boring.

Waverly Mansion has become more of a community since Urquhart started making the videos. Everyone can participate, whether on their feet or in a wheelchair, and participate they do.

Urquhart's YouTube scheme honors creativity and zest for life. She recognizes the seniors at Waverly Mansion as people with gifts to share. The world needs more Sarah Urquharts, people who understand that physical infirmities do not automatically mean mental decline.

Read more:
- Sarah Urquhart's YouTube channel for Waverly Mansion — https://goo.gl/ozbJRF
- "A 'Play with a Purpose' Program Shows The Waverly Mansion to the World"— http://goo.gl/jSwIX2
- "Local Retirement Residents Create Valentine's Video after YouTube Videos Go Viral"— https://goo.gl/7Fsg1r

Dementia in Denmark

People with advanced dementia in the U.S. and Canada generally end up in convalescent homes, where their freedoms are severely limited.

Denmark takes a different approach. In that country elders with dementia have a right to decide how they want to live. They go on holidays, ride bicycles, chop wood, and fall in love. They decide how they will spend their days. The idea is to keep them active and integrated in the community as long as possible.

Alzheimer Europe says Danes with dementia are protected by government policy which states that "the patient's dignity, integrity and right of self-determination must be respected."

Lotte, a care home in Copenhagen, is the residence often referred to as the gold standard. When artist Lucy Lyons went there in November 2010 to draw experiences of aging, she was impressed by how non-institutional it felt, with linen, china and cutlery on the dining tables, wine and beer with meals, and an atmosphere of warmth.

Denmark used to warehouse people, as too many other countries still do. But Thyra Frank, a nurse and member of parliament, worked tirelessly to change that. Today Denmark's elderly lead active lives, in whatever ways they can, until they die. The system is designed to support seniors, not take away their independence.

That sounds like a recipe for keeping people healthier longer, and the healthier we are, the less of a strain we are on our medical systems. Denmark's elder care is a model of compassion and respect. North Americans can learn a lot from it.

Read more:
- OK House Lotte website — http://okhjemmetlotte.dk/
- "'Dementia Village' Inspires New Care"— http://goo.gl/o12ed5
- "Dutch Village Offers Dignified Care for Dementia Sufferers"— http://goo.gl/JCRnda

TimeSlips, Storytelling within Dementia

A wheelchair-bound man who yearned to be a storyteller was one of the first people to send me to the Internet to find out all I could about various forms of memory loss and dementia. His short-term memory emptied its contents every few minutes. He could not learn new stories. What he discovered in the personal-stories workshop I was teaching was that his long-term memory was a bottomless treasure. With his natural flair for engaging an audience, he could make a compelling tale out of an ordinary event.

What the treasure box of old memories did for this man, TimeSlips has been doing since 1996 for people whose stories have disappeared down the well of dementia. Anne Basting, then Director of the Center on Age and Community at the University of Wisconsin Milwaukee, started it to make life better for people with dementia. She wanted to replace the pressure to remember with the encouragement to imagine.

She knew that as people undergo memory loss, they begin to self-censor. They fear they might say the wrong thing. Worse yet, they might say something that would lead to their losing independence. Basting wanted them to have the pleasure of communication without the worry of consequences. In a TimeSlips workshop, they could start with a story prompt and take it in any direction.

The stories participants tell can be shared with families, e-mailed to friends and posted on blogs. They shift the focus from what people with dementia have lost to what they can still create.

TimeSlips has gone global and has trained over 2,000 facilitators. More than 30 facilities and organizations have embedded the method in their activities programs. Online training is available.

Dementia touches everyone's life in one way or another. TimeSlips is a respectful and creative way of honoring people's gifts, whatever they may be.

Read more:
- TimeSlips website — http://www.timeslips.org/
- "Alzheimer's Patients Turn to Stories Instead of Memories"— http://goo.gl/8wJ0hr
- "Impact of TimeSlips" — http://goo.gl/dIAZB6

The Best Way to Avoid Alzheimer's

When Jay Ingram came to Kelowna, B.C., to talk about the science of Alzheimer's, tickets quickly disappeared and the University of British Columbia Okanagan rented a nearby theater for a second night.

His talk was far from reassuring. The increase in life expectancy has led to an accompanying uptick in Alzheimer's. We are a long way from knowing how to prevent or treat the disease. The implications are staggering when we consider that past the age of 85, the odds of developing Alzheimer's or some other dementia rise to 50 percent.

Still, two things in his talk gave the audience hope. One was that education is a preventive strategy. People with more education are less likely to get dementia. Given what families and health care systems pay for dementia care, this seems a good argument for spending the money upfront. If all young people receive the best possible education, at the other end of their lives they will have a better chance of avoiding the high cost of failing brains.

Ingram also said exercise has preventive properties. A 40-minute walk, every day of the week, appears to reduce risks. A healthy diet and socializing with friends are also factors, but that daily walk is key.

Now I have one more reason to celebrate my very walkable neighborhood. While I am picking up a library book, going to a play, buying groceries, listening to a lecture or photographing the nearby marsh, I will tell myself it is all part of a prescription to keep my brain healthy.

Read more:
- "Living in the Cloud of Alzheimer's"— http://goo.gl/EZTNiR
- 2015 Alzheimer's Disease Facts and Figures — http://www.alz.org/facts/overview.asp

The Greek Island of Vigorous Old Age

People who live on Ikaria, a small, remote Aegean island 35 miles off the coast of Turkey, enjoy the good life. They eat a Mediterranean diet, drink home-made wine, and spend hours chatting with friends. They live simply, spend a lot of time outdoors, and get plenty of exercise walking up and down the island's hills. An unusually high percentage live beyond their 100th birthdays, and they have an average life span ten years longer than other Europeans.

BBC's Andrew Bomford interviewed the island's "poster child" for a piece published January 6, 2013, "The Greek island of old age". He wrote about Stamatis Moraitis, who turned 98 on New Year's Day 2013. Although born on Ikaria, Stamatis was living in the U.S. when he was diagnosed with terminal lung cancer. Told he had nine months to live, he returned to Ikaria to die. Every day he and his friends got together to drink wine. Moraitis grew stronger by the day. When he spoke to Bomford, he had outlived the diagnosis by 45 years.

Daily Mail writer Jan Moir met Evangelia Karnava, born in March 1913, on Ikaria. The 100-year-old woman was taking daily walks to local shops, using the latest technology and living on her own. She told Moir her one diet secret was not eating red meat, though she did eat the fat.

Stories like these raise questions for scientists and doctors studying factors that extend or shorten life. A study published in *Cardiology Research and Practice* looked at Ikarians over the age of 80. The researchers found a higher percentage of over-90s compared with the rest of Europe. Most of them were physically active, had healthy diets, avoided smoking, socialized a lot, and took naps. Depression was rare among them.

Dan Buettner was also curious about the Ikarians. He partnered with National Geographic to study the island as part of his work identifying why people live longer in what he dubbed the world's Blue Zones. He identified active lifestyles and healthy diets as major contributors, but what set the Ikarians apart was the tight-knit community. Over the centuries they had developed a culture in which optimism and sociability were embedded in the fabric of daily life.

People have a sense of belonging on Ikaria. They know they are important members of the community. Everyone is. What the Ikarians receive in exchange for living more simply is a high quality of life that does not require big incomes or a lot of possessions.

We cannot all move to Ikaria, but we can learn from the islanders, not just to live longer but to live better.

Read more:
- "The Greek Island of Old Age"— http://www.bbc.com/news/magazine-20898379
- "The Island of (Almost) Eternal Life"— http://goo.gl/WP64nb
- "Sociodemographic and Lifestyle Statistics of Oldest People Living in Ikaria Island"— http://goo.gl/ZIRh6R
- "The Island Where People Forget to Die"— http://goo.gl/RhQw4n

Credits

Cover: Cover photo: "Elderly Gentlemen" by Lucia Whittaker, via Flickr Creative Commons

Poem: "That Old Man Hiding in My Mirror" by Rick Hardman, used with author's permission

Part 1 – No Time for Bad Days: Sunset over Lake Okanagan, photo by Cathryn Wellner

Quote from *The Velveteen Rabbit* by Margery Williams, in "Aging into Love and Loving into Age," public domain

Part 2 – Creative to the End: "Boats", painting by Hilda Gorenstein (Hilgos), used by permission of the Hilgos Foundation

Part 3 – A Bridge between Old and Young: Grandparent and granddaughter, down by the sea, photo by Cathryn Wellner

Part 4 – Never Too Old: Autumn Leaves, photo by Cathryn Wellner

Part 5 – Feisty Aging: Edith Macefield's house, photo by Ban Tesch, via Wikimedia Commons

Part 6 – Parts of Me Still Work: Robin Jarman walking by the sea, photo by Cathryn Wellner

About the author

Cathryn Wellner is a writer and photographer who can usually be found either staring at her computer screen or taking her camera for a walk. She is on a hunt for what is right with the world and blogs about the  creative, generous, brilliant, kind, inventive people who are making a mark on the planet.

She is venturing back into the print and e-book world with the whimsical photo stories of *Turtle Talk* (http://cathrynwellner.com/blog), the *Hope Wins* series (http://thisgivesmehope.com/books), and a forthcoming memoir, *The Reluctant Farmer*.

Contact her at cathryn@cathrynwellner.com, on Twitter (@StoryRoute), Facebook (at This Gives Me Hope) or via her website, http://cathrynwellner.com.

Acknowledgments

To all of the people included in this book, I owe a debt of gratitude. You are extraordinary models for aging with zest and spirit.

Those who agreed to read and comment on the draft deserve special thanks. You took time out of your busy lives to assist me. Robin Jarman was the first reader, then Lisa Wagner and Sharon Currie, who read line by line as only a terrific copy editor can do. Thank you, Kathleen Ellis, Julie McIntyre, Lisa Wagner, and Donna Houghtalin, for your kind comments and to all the fellow SARKers (a global group of creatives who have connected through workshops with Susan Ariel Rainbow Kennedy) whose encouragement buoys me on a daily basis.

Also by Cathryn Wellner

Turn lemons into lemonade, with stories that show how Hope Wins and ordinary people can change the world.

Links to this and all of Cathryn's other books can be found at http://www.cathrynwellner.com/cathryns-books/

Thanks & a request

Readers are the best kinds of people. Book buyers are in the angel category. Your purchase of this book helps keep the hope coming. It is available in digital and print versions. If you bought the print version, send a copy of your receipt to cathryn@cathrynwellner.com, and I will send you a free copy of the PDF e-book, which has all kinds of hyperlinks embedded in it, as well as many more photographs.

If you enjoyed this book in the Hope Wins series, please post a review on Goodreads or Amazon or iTunes or anywhere you prefer. Send a copy to cathryn@cathrynwellner.com to receive the next e-book (PDF format) in the series free.

Made in the USA
San Bernardino, CA
11 December 2016